The Developing Child

Recent decades have witnessed unprecedented advances in research on human development. In those same decades there have been profound changes in public policy toward children. Each book in the Developing Child series reflects the importance of such research in its own right and as it bears on the formulation of policy. It is the purpose of the series to make the findings of this research available to those who are responsible for raising a new generation and for shaping policy in its behalf. We hope that these books will provide rich and useful information for parents, educators, child-care professionals, students of developmental psychology, and all others concerned with the challenge of human growth.

Jerome Bruner
New York University
Michael Cole
University of California, San Diego
SERIES EDITORS

The Developing Child Series

Infancy

Tiffany Field

Harvard University Press
Cambridge, Massachusetts
London, England   1990

Library of Congress Cataloging-in-Publication Data

Field, Tiffany.
  Infancy / Tiffany Field.
      p.   cm.—(The Developing child)
  Includes bibliographical references and index.
  ISBN 0-674-45262-3 (cloth).—ISBN 0-674-45263-1 (pbk.)
  1. Infant psychology.   I. Title.   II. Series.
BF719.F53   1990   90-37566
155.42'2—dc20   CIP

To my parents, Betty and Harvey Martini,
my daughter, Tory, and her father, Barry,
for the most memorable infancies

Contents

Preface

The reason for writing this volume was to describe how amazing infants have turned out to be. Although there are earlier studies on infants, it is only during the last two decades that we have come to appreciate the sophistication and the complex development of the infant. Many parents are still surprised when they realize a newborn can see and hear. Imagine our surprise, then, when we discovered that newborns could do many more things: recognize their mother's face and voice, imitate facial expressions, add simple numbers, and even discriminate the sounds of music—to name only a few of their extraordinary abilities. Imagine how much more they can do as they explore the world and develop relationships.

This volume tries to cover as much of this exciting information as possible in a very small space. I have focused primarily on social-emotional development, which is my research area. However, I have also tried to give a feeling for the perceptual, cognitive, and motor development of the infant since all of these developments are inextricably entangled. Because so much happens even before birth an account is given of the development of the fetus, and because some 10 percent of us have infants at risk there is a chapter on those infants. In addition, although many examples come from our own research, I have tried to present extensive and up-to-date references so that students as well as parents might find this volume useful.

I owe much of the inspiration for this volume to three children whose infancies I can remember: my sister Mary, a friend's daughter Loren, and my own daughter Tory. The first infancy I experienced at eight years of age and the latter two during graduate school, when I was taking care of the babies, videotaping them in every conceivable situation, and generally being entertained by their behavior. Tory's father, Barry, made the experience even more fun. Around that time I also received grant monies to study the longitudinal development of hundreds of preterm and post-term infants as well as infants of teenage mothers. While the babies I helped raise taught me that infants are extremely sophisticated, the high-risk infants showed me how resilient and invulnerable they can be. Since that time our neonatal intensive care nurseries and follow-up clinics have constantly presented new problems to be studied, and our nursery school has continually impressed me with how infants can thrive in exciting environments.

There are countless infants and parents I want to thank for these experiences. I am also very grateful to my mentors Laura Joseph, Anita Olds, Rachel Clifton, and Michael Nelson, and to my many colleagues for their inspiration and collaboration. I am indebted to Jean Greer and Jennifer Snodgrass for helping with the manuscript of this book.

Finally, I want to thank the many undergraduate, graduate, and postdoctoral students who shared wonderful ideas and helped immensely with all the research we did; their names are on our articles in the reference lists.

My hope is that reading this book will be half as enjoyable for you as studying and writing about infancy has been for me.

The
Developing
Child

Infancy

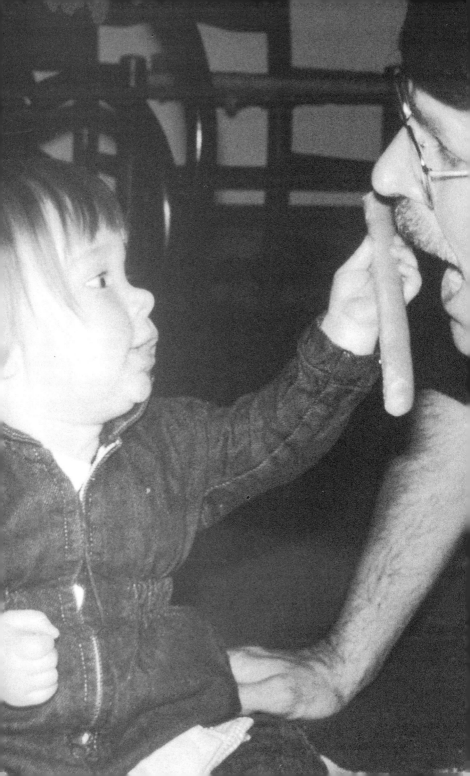

1 / Studying Infants

The word "infancy" means the period without language. Thus, infancy covers the first two years of life
before language emerges. People study infants for different reasons. Some view infancy as an optimal testing
ground for heredity-environment or nature-nurture
questions. Others view it as the first stage in human
development. The recent popularity of the field suggests that infants are gradually becoming viewed as
worthy of study simply because they are interesting.

The development of methods for studying infants has
proceeded more slowly. Infancy as a field of study, like
its parent, developmental psychology, adopted a number of experimental psychology paradigms from other
fields. Methods were borrowed from animal, child, and
adult laboratory studies. Although rigorous methods
may contribute to the field's status in the scientific com-
munity, some infancy researchers have been concerned
about developing more ecologically meaningful methods such as naturalistic observations.

Observations of infants like those recorded by Darwin
and Piaget were instrumental in establishing infancy as
an area of study and provided inspiration for many laboratory studies (Darwin 1877; Piaget 1952). However,
their naturalistic observation method has not been

1

widely accepted as a research paradigm. As many as 80 percent of all developmental investigations have been conducted in the laboratory. Because of this, many interesting behaviors of infants that lend themselves more readily to naturalistic observation—such as the exploration of objects by mouth, pointing gestures, and "container" behaviors—have not yet been researched. In an appeal for more naturalistic observation research, one developmental psychologist wrote that "A case can be made that the description of relationships in naturalistic environments, while not sufficient to establish that factor X does cause behavior Y, is necessary for such a conclusion . . . We rarely take the time to keep our experimental hands off a behavior long enough to make descriptive observations in naturalistic settings of the several dimensions and circumstances of the behavior we wish to study" (McCall 1977).

The laboratory approach derives from a world view that studies infancy to answer nature-nurture questions or to understand evolving psychological processes. Naturalistic observation, in contrast, is directed at describing the behavior that occurs in natural settings, as Darwin did with infants and with many other animal species, and Piaget did with his own infants in an attempt to develop an epistemology of the mind. It is appropriate that their behavioral descriptions be empirically tested in the laboratory. However, most laboratory experiments have involved investigations of how the infant responds to what is provided rather than what the infant spontaneously does. Both approaches are critical to the field. One describes a phenomenon, whereas the other empirically assesses the phenomenon.

Another orientation in the field of infancy is the search for predictors of later development. Sigmund

Freud and John B. Watson, as well as other developmental psychologists, assume that experiences beginning in infancy are critical for later development (Freud 1949; Watson 1928). Freud asserted that trauma during a particular stage of infancy would cause fixation, for example at the oral or anal stage, precluding development to the next stage and affecting personality characteristics such as temperament. Watson similarly believed that infants subjected to early conditioning experiences would carry the effects throughout life. Freud considered these effects reversible through therapy involving free association and dream analysis designed to analyze their earliest origins. Watson similarly considered early experiences reversible through counterconditioning techniques.

Retrospective reconstruction of events tends to confirm a linear developmental model such as Watson's or Freud's. For example, many cerebral palsied and mentally retarded infants are found to have been subjected to a variety of adverse perinatal conditions, such as lack of oxygen. However, studies suggest that many infants experience perinatal complications but do not develop palsy or mental retardation. An additional criticism of Freud and the psychoanalytic tradition is that the infant does not appear to pass through oral or anal stages, so it is not clear how fixation could occur (Stern, 1985).

For many developmental psychologists, the failure to find continuity has given rise to theories that propose that infancy is discontinuous with later developmental stages and therefore a less critical stage of development than previously thought. As Kagan and others have suggested, the developmental course of individual infants may not be linear or even unidirectional; given the multitude of interactional events that occur, there is little reason to expect to make predictions from this earliest period (Kagan et al. 1978). Lipsitt, however, has pointed out that this need not mean that there is little or no continuity between earlier conditions or experiences and later events (Lipsitt 1988). He enters two caveats: First, the overpowering or reversing effects of later experiences on a seemingly preset condition do not diminish the importance of the earlier condition. Second, the structure of behavior sometimes disguises underlying commonalities in experience; noncontinuities can be examples of continuities not yet sufficiently investigated.

Still another orientation is the highly specialized focus on psychological processes during infancy. There are problems with transferring the study of a specific process, such as memory, to the infancy stage. Unlike memory at later stages, it cannot be isolated and studied independent of perceptual, attentional, and physiological processes. Alertness, attention, perception, information processing, and remembering are not very easily separated in infants. In addition, memory is rapidly developing, so that infant memory may look very different at six months than it did at three months. Psychological processes (which by definition occur across time) are rarely longitudinally studied across infancy in the true developmental sense.

Among the methodological challenges posed for the infant researcher, then, are the needs to observe the infant's natural behaviors, to study evolving processes in the context of other related processes, and to track these longitudinally across infancy. Other methodological problems are posed by the infants themselves.

MEASURES OF INFANT RESPONSE

The infant's inability to communicate and limited response repertoire are perhaps the most serious of the problems. An infant is unable to communicate verbally perceptions, thoughts, and feelings. In the absence of language, researchers have relied on motor and physiological responses. Among these are simple reflex behaviors, such as sucking, and voluntary behaviors, such as head turning and looking. Heart rate is the most popularly used physiological measure. Other responses that are less frequently used in the laboratory but are often recorded during naturalistic observations include eye widening, smiling, grimacing, laughing, and cooing.

Sucking, a universal activity most infants enjoy, starts in utero and continues throughout infancy. Infants can be trained at a very early stage to suck a pacifier more or less vigorously in response to the reinforcers that researchers provide (Figure 1.1). Problems with using this measure are that many breastfed babies will not suck on a pacifier; sucking often ceases when the infant's attention is captured by something else; and sucking may affect other measures being recorded. An infant who is preoccupied with sucking will often refuse to attend to other stimulation (Bruner 1973). In addition, sucking confounds the measurement of heart rate due to its "driving" effect on heart rate (Nelson et al. 1978). Head turning is also a very common behavior in the early repertoire of the infant and can be easily trained. It, too, has problems because most infants have a head-turning preference, typically to the right side.

Despite these problems, there are many ways these behaviors can show us what the infant knows or feels. For example, head turning can indicate the infant's ability to discriminate sounds coming from different directions and intensity of sucking can indicate which liquids the infant prefers. An example of a more sophisticated behavior is the newborn's ability to learn to suck for

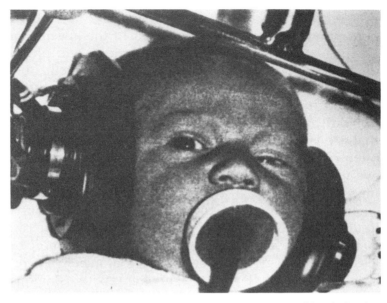

Figure 1.1. Newborn infant learning to change its sucking behavior to hear its mother's voice.

shorter periods of time when the reinforcement is hearing its mother read Dr. Seuss's "And to Think That I Saw It on Mulberry Street" rather than hearing a stranger read the same book (DeCasper and Fifer 1980). From that behavior we can infer that the newborn recognizes and prefers its mother's voice.

Looking behavior or visual fixations are other frequently used measures. They can be reliably recorded from corneal reflections either through peepholes or by using infrared photography. They are typically used to measure attention, preference, and habituation. Habituation, the most primitive form of learning, is shown by a reduced response after repeated exposure to a stimulus. An illustration of the ways in which an infant can show attention, preference, and habituation comes from a study we conducted on newborns' discrimination of their mothers' faces during the first day of life. If a mother's and a stranger's face are alternately presented to a newborn through a trapdoor on a stimulus box, the newborn will look for a longer time at the mother's face, suggesting an initial preference (Field et al. 1983). If the mother's face is then presented over a series of trials, the infant will look less and less at the mother's face. Once the newborn has become habituated to the mother's face, the newborn looks at the stranger's face for longer periods than the mother's face. One of the problems with the use of visual fixations is how to interpret them. If they are used as an index of preference, then longer visual fixations on a novel stimulus would be viewed as evidence of preference and of the infant having processed a previously presented (familiar) stimulus. If, however, they are used as an index of habituation, the longer visual fixations or the infants' failure to cease looking at the stimulus would be interpreted as a failure to learn.

In addition, the duration of looking appears to differ with the nature of the stimulus. Novelty, complexity, and movement are among the many qualities that affect the amount of time an infant looks at something. Infants often prolong their gaze at inanimate stimuli whereas they alternate looking toward and away from an animate stimulus. The longer fixations on the inanimate stimulus could be interpreted as a preference; yet other studies show that infants are attracted to animate stimulation. This illustrates the problem of drawing conclusions from a single behavior such as looking. Sometimes adding another measure, such as heart rate, gives us more information.

Heart rate is one of the most frequently employed physiological measures in the study of infants. Heart rate decelerations occur when the infant is attentive or orienting toward the stimulus (Graham and Clifton 1966). Heart rate accelerations are noted when aversive or uninteresting stimuli are presented. Heart rate is one of the few measures that can be used for indicating what is being perceived and learned during sleep, which is the way infants spend most of their time. Unfortunately, when infants are awake their heart rate is affected by other behaviors: for example, sucking causes the heart rate to rise; the infant's movements can affect heart rate; and fussing, crying, and gaze averting also tend to elevate heart rate (Nelson et al. 1978).

It is important to look at the infant's behavior while recording heart rate. For example, heart rate accelerations (instead of the expected decelerations) have been known to occur when the infant is exposed to very interesting stimulation, only because the infant, unknown to the experimenter, was sleeping throughout the experiment. In an experiment with three-month-old infants we recorded heart rate responses to an arrangement of moving Christmas tree lights. Curiously, the infants did not show heart rate decelerations, which would indicate attentiveness. Although the dancing lights had captivated the adults' attention, the infants were lulled to sleep by them.

Other problems associated with the use of heart rate include changes in a given state. For example, heart rate is higher in active than in quiet alert states and in active than in quiet sleep. Further, there are developmental shifts in both overall heart rate (it slows down across development) and directional changes (acceleration or deceleration). It is very difficult to elicit deceleration in newborns, although it is a common response of a one-month-old to a novel stimulus.

Crying is another behavior that can be used to interpret the infant's intentions. Different cry patterns signal pain, hunger, discomfort, and boredom. Darwin perhaps provided one of the first observations of this phenomenon, not from the sound patterns that are more typically researched today but from the facial expressions of crying infants (Figure 1.2): "Infants, when suffering even slight pain, moderate hunger, or discomfort, utter violent and prolonged screams. Whilst thus screaming their eyes are firmly closed, so that the skin round them is wrinkled, and the forehead contracted into a frown. The mouth is widely opened with the lips retracted in a peculiar manner, which causes it to assume a squarish form; the gums or teeth being more or less exposed."

Darwin trusted that the infants' facial expressions reflected their states of mind: "In order to acquire as good a foundation as possible, and to ascertain, independently of common opinion, how far particular movements of the features and gestures are really expressive of certain states of the mind, I have found the following means the most serviceable. In the first place, to observe infants; for they exhibit many emotions, as Sir C. Bell remarks, 'with extraordinary force'; whereas, in after life, some of our expressions cease to have the pure and simple source from which they sprang in infancy" (Darwin 1965, p. 147).

FINDING INTERESTING STIMULI
AND OPTIMAL STATES

It is important to use stimulation infants find interesting, in order to gain their attention and get them to perform. Attention and motivation depend on qualities such as novelty, complexity, intensity, and animation. Colored paper forms, for example, may be less interest-

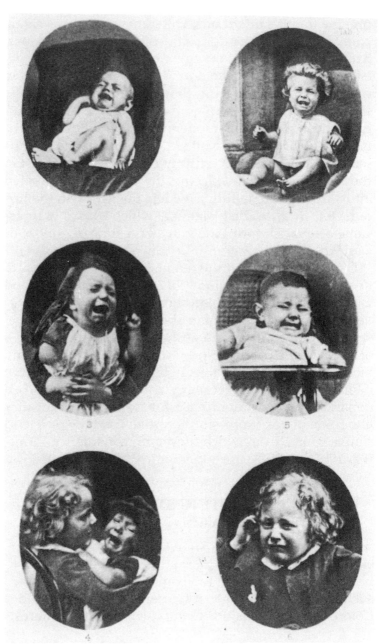

Figure 1.2. Photographs of infant crying expressions from Darwin's *The Expression of the Emotions in Man and Animals.*

ing to the infant than moving colored lights. Many erroneous conclusions about infant capabilities have probably been drawn from situations in which uninteresting stimuli were used. The researcher may mistakenly attribute the absence of a response to limitations of the infant rather than to an uninteresting stimulus. If infants seem to prefer a human face to a bull's eye, or the mother's voice to pure tones, or an animate to an inanimate stimulus, then perceptual processes may be measured more effectively with these stimuli (Fantz 1966; Hutt et al. 1968). In addition, fewer infants may fall asleep during experiments.

Another important problem to consider is the change in abilities and agendas of the infant. The interest value of stimuli and the significance of responses are affected by shifting state organization, sensorimotor abilities, and developmental agendas of the infant. Sleep-wake cycles shift dramatically, particularly during stages of rapid physiological change and brain maturation, for example at six and twelve weeks (Parmelee and Stern 1972; Dittrichova and Lapackova 1964). Sensorimotor abilities also change as noted in observations and shown by infant assessments such as the Bayley scales. Changes in visual perception and information processing abilities, for example, may explain the shift from the infant's preference for real faces at birth to a preference for scrambled faces at eight months (Goren et al. 1975; Kagan 1967). Similarly, if grasping is used as the primary response and the infant cannot yet grasp an object effectively, we cannot conclude that the infant does not intend to reach the object. When infants are preoccupied with their own developmental activities, they are not likely to be interested in performing for a parent or a researcher. If infants are currently working on walking or talking skills, as is typical at twelve months, they may not be amenable to sitting still for an attention task, just as six-month-olds are less interested in face-to-face interactions with their mothers since they are typically preoccupied with manipulating objects.

One of the biggest problems in studying infants—the one we call the culprit variable—is that an infant may fall asleep or go on a crying jag in the middle of an observation. Given that infant states (sleeping or waking, fussing or laughing) are so highly variable, particularly during the early months, we often must wait to observe the infant at the infant's optimal time. Many researchers claim that midway between feedings is an alert time, whereas others consider the period immediately before feeding as optimal (Brazelton 1973; Pomerleau-Malcuit and Clifton 1973). Just before feeding infants are often more alert but sometimes fussy because they are hungry; immediately after feeding they may be less fussy but also more sleepy because they have just fed. Despite considerable efforts to determine the infant's optimal state, the dropout rate in infant studies because of drowsiness or fussiness is often around 50 percent. Researchers who study sleep states experience lower dropout rates, although even then infants are often in the wrong sleep state. High dropout rates may bias the results of studies since the infants who remain tend to be more alert and less fussy than those who drop out.

Fussiness is typically solved by giving the infant a pacifier. However, sucking affects heart rate and may reduce the infant's interest in other stimulation. One of the most popular ways to reduce infant fussiness or drowsiness is to hold the infant in a face-to-face position, bob up and down with a few deep knee bends, and make clicking sounds. This combination of movement and auditory stimulation often helps the infant reach an alert state. For the first few months infants are typically more alert when held upright on an adult's shoulder or face-to-face. At three months they are alert when placed in an infant seat, but by six months they no longer tolerate it, preferring a high chair, jumper, or walker. Usually the infant will give all of the cues necessary to indicate whether he or she is in an optimal state.

Aside from observations and laboratory experiments, much has been learned about the infant from parents. Parents have been a source of information for countless studies, probably because they are most familiar with their infants' behavior and can report on a broader sampling of behavior. Inventories have been designed to record parents' perceptions of behaviors, including the MABI (Mother's Assessment of the Behavior of her Infant), infant temperament inventories, behavior diaries, activity records, and developmental assessment scales (Field et al. 1978). Parents must also keep in mind such important considerations as observing the infant in his optimal state, finding the most interesting stimulus, and looking for the most reliable responses.

Infants, by virtue of their limited periods of wakefulness and rapidly changing skills and interests, pose a large number of challenging problems for those who study them. Despite these problems, infants frequently surprise researchers and parents by their competence. Even without language, they can tell us a great deal. Convergent methods (such as naturalistic and laboratory observations) and multiple measures (such as visual behavior, heart rate, and parents' reports) can help overcome some of the unique problems encountered in studying infants.

An example of a multidimensional, multimeasure approach is the study of imitation. The infant's imitation

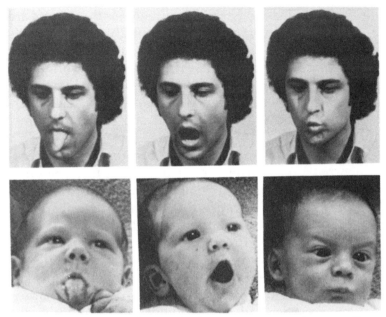

Figure 1.3. Newborn infants imitating tongue protrusion, mouth opening, and lip pursing.

abilities are the source of considerable debate in the literature. Darwin presented some of the first descriptions of facial expression mimicry in the context of discussing the universality of facial expressions. Piaget did not observe true imitation in his children until late in the first year. More recently Piaget's students successfully elicited imitations of facial expressions with newborn infants. These naturalistic observations ultimately led to laboratory manipulations that succeeded in documenting neonatal imitation, especially in infants who could be aroused to an optimal state (see Figure 1.3; Meltzoff and Moore 1977; Gardner and Gardner 1970; Maratos 1973).

Much of the infant's development, such as learning to

mimic facial expressions, occurs in a social-emotional context. Language develops in the context of social interactions. The understanding that objects are permanent and the fear of strangers also depend on social interaction for their development. Because social-emotional development is one of the most important areas of infancy and because it is a critical foundation for later processes such as language, this volume has a strong orientation toward social-emotional development. In the next chapter social-emotional developments such as neonatal recognition of the mother, imitation, and bonding to the parent will be discussed. In the subsequent chapters data will be reviewed on the discrimination of emotional expressions, on social interactions with parents and peers, and on early attachments. The final chapter gives examples of infants at risk for developmental delays because of inadequate stimulation and discusses how interventions can facilitate social-emotional development.

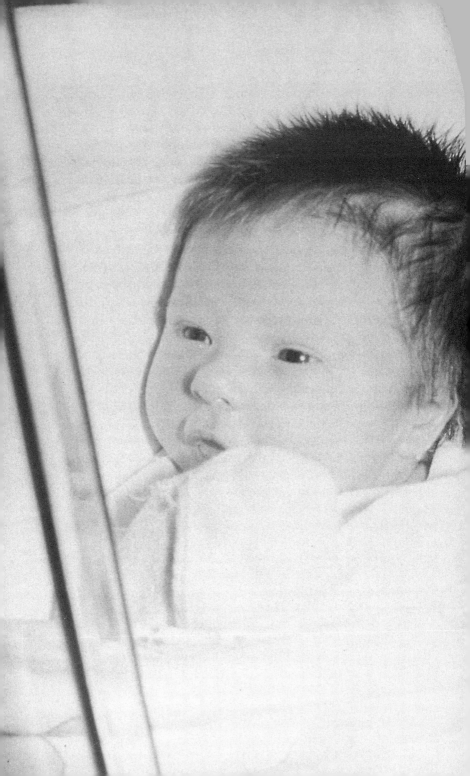

2/ Before and After Birth

During the first three months of pregnancy the embryo develops most of its vital organs and physiological systems. By the end of this period the face, fingers, toes, and genitalia are already present. From three months onward, the musculature and the central nervous system develop rapidly. By the end of the fourth month movements can be felt by the mother and the fetal heartbeat can be detected. By the end of five months reflexes such as sucking, swallowing, and hiccuping are usually present. By the sixth month nails, sweat glands, and skin have developed, and the eyes can open and close (Fischer and Lazerson 1984). Around this time survival becomes probable in the event of a premature delivery.

PERCEPTION AND BEHAVIOR BEFORE BIRTH

Our knowledge of fetal growth, development, perception, and behavior has been significantly enhanced in the last decade by the development of fetal ultrasonography. In the ultrasound examination, a probe applied to the mother's skin sends acoustic pulses into the body where they are deflected at various angles by bones and by tissues of different densities. The image on the video screen is synthesized from the reflected pulses, with the strongest signals (those that reflect high densities) appearing as white and nonreflecting areas appearing as black (Birnholz and Farrell 1984). In many European countries ultrasound examinations are standard prenatal care, while in the United States they are still confined largely to high-risk pregnancies. These examinations can reduce parents' anxiety, and some have even claimed they enhance parent-infant bonding.

We know from ultrasonography that by the end of the first trimester of pregnancy the fetus spends much of its time moving. By the middle of pregnancy the mother reports feeling these movements. The amniotic fluid and the length of the umbilical cord allow for considerable flexibility of movement. At first the movements look uncontrolled and the fetus is likely to spend as much time with its head up as with it down. But by mid-pregnancy the movements are more controlled and the head is more likely to be down. Using ultrasound, several different behaviors can be distinguished, including startles, generalized movements of the head and trunk, regular and irregular breathing, jaw movements including rhythmical mouthing, and eye movements associated with rapid eye movement (REM) sleep and deep sleep. Hiccups, yawns, sucking, and swallowing are also frequently noted. Slow eye movements are present as early as sixteen weeks; rapid eye movements begin at around twenty-three weeks and continue up to around thirty-six weeks, when long periods of quiet sleep are noted (Birnholz 1981).

Prior to ultrasonography, fetal researchers depended upon aborted fetuses to determine capabilities of the fetus (Humphrey 1969). These studies reported the presence very early in gestation of fetal reflexes such as rooting (turning the cheek toward a tactile stimulus), sucking, hand-to-mouth activity, grasping, and reflexes of the feet. These investigators also noted facial expressions such as disgust, sadness, fear, and happiness in the fetus. Thus, ultrasonographers were not surprised when these kinds of facial expressions appeared on their video screens.

We can intuit some of what the fetus senses from its behavior. That the fetus can tumble around in utero and move in a fairly coordinated way suggests that it senses movement (vestibular stimulation) and has a sense of balance. The data on aborted fetuses showing reflexive responses to simple touch suggest that the fetus has a well-developed sense of touch. It is not surprising that these sensory systems are developed, given the significant opportunities for motion and tactile stimulation in utero. We also presume that the fetus has a sense of taste since it has a multitude of taste buds. Because a newborn within hours of birth shows the ability to discriminate sweetness, sourness, and bitterness, we presume that it can at least taste these different flavors toward the end of gestation (Steiner 1979). The fetus may experience these flavors by tasting the amniotic fluid, which comprises several sugars, salts, and acids.

The most popularly investigated sensory system in the fetus is hearing. Most mothers would attest to its hearing ability based on increased fetal activity when they are in presence of loud noises or music. The loud vibrations of the mother's internal organs, including the heart, the intestines, and the lungs, have led several to speculate that the womb is a very noisy place. However, since liquid is not a very effective medium for transmitting sound, and because the outer ears of the fetus are protected by a creamy substance called vernix, it is unlikely that sounds are perceived by the fetus at full intensity. In addition, several researchers have noted that the fetus appears to habituate to most sounds. The fetus typically responds by movement and accelerated heart rate, which diminish following the repetition of the sound. When a new sound is presented the fetus starts responding again. Fetal movement and habituation are reported to relate to later infant behavior and development (Gelman et al. 1982).

Sound that is delivered by a commercial vibrator placed on the maternal abdomen is more effective in eliciting a response from the fetus than air-borne noise played through a speaker placed approximately a foot from the maternal abdomen (Kisilevsky and Muir 1987). This suggests that the mother's internal sounds and voice are more readily perceived by the fetus than sounds from the external environment. (This is not to suggest, however, that commercial vibrators be used for fetal stimulation; they may have unknown harmful effects.) The mother's voice that the fetus hears presumably would be very different from the voice the newborn hears. Nonetheless, in one study newborns recognized their mother's voice after having heard it read a story during the last weeks of pregnancy (DeCasper and Fifer 1980). In addition, newborns that had a choice between hearing the story that had been read to them during the last weeks of pregnancy and another story, chose the story they had heard during pregnancy. Furthermore, the newborn appears to recognize the mother's voice before it recognizes its father's voice, suggesting that perhaps the patterns and rhythms of her voice come to be familiar to the fetus (DeCasper and Prescott 1984).

The womb might be described as a place of blooming, buzzing confusion. Despite the disquiet and discomfort, the fetus grows and develops more in these months than during any other period of life. After tumbling about, feeling, tasting, and hearing, it is no wonder that the emerging newborn is so well prepared for the out-side world.

THE BIRTH PROCESS

The birth of a baby is one of those experiences that parents never forget. Some have claimed that even the baby does not forget. Childbirth preparation classes and the assistance of fathers have made delivery a happier experience. The mother with a supportive companion experiences shorter labor and fewer problems with de-livery (Sosa et al 1980).

The long process of labor and delivery must feel like sensory bombardment for the fetus. However, the fetus supposedly feels less pain than the mother because it is being squeezed while the mother is being stretched. The mother may ask for pain relief or the obstetrician may give her relief without her asking. Newborns whose mothers received moderate to heavy doses of anesthesia or analgesics during labor show general neo-natal depression, behavioral disorganization, and dis-turbed feeding responses (Lester et al. 1982; Murray et al. 1981). Attention and motor abilities are impaired at least during the first month of age. Low levels of med-ication appear to have negligible effects on infant be-havior. Of course, any negative effects might result from the difficult interaction of the mother with a depressed, unresponsive infant. The neonate's depressed behavior may contribute to increased maternal anxiety, but it may also be that the most anxious mothers need higher lev-els of medication during labor and delivery. Despite these short-term effects, however, there appear to be no longer-term effects of obstetrical medication.

Because pain is considered a learned phenomenon, and since very little learning is attributed to newborns, they are sometimes considered unable to experience pain as we know it during delivery. At least they are thought not to remember the pain because they have very limited memory skills. However, the newborn does emerge from the birth canal crying; and because new-born infants cry during invasive procedures such as heelsticks and circumcision, we assume that they do experience pain at this very early stage.

Despite the potential pain, the infant's experience of labor is important for normal breathing. The production of a substance that lines the lungs, called surfactant, is stimulated by the contractions of the uterus. Babies who are delivered by elective Caesarean section, and there-fore do not experience the contractions, produce less surfactant and are more vulnerable to breathing prob-lems than babies who are delivered vaginally or even babies who experience some hours of labor before being delivered by Caesarean. However, there are compen-sating advantages to Caesarean delivery, beyond avoid-ing medical complications. One is that the father becomes more involved in early caregiving, perhaps be-cause he typically receives the newborn first while the mother is recovering from surgery (Field and Widmayer 1981; Gewirtz and Hollenbeck 1989; Kochanevich-Wallace et al. 1988).

THE FIRST MOMENTS OF LIFE

The first moments of life must seem very cold and very bright to the newborn, who has been accustomed to warmth and darkness. The temperature inside the uterus is both higher and less variable than that of the rest of the mother's body. The newborn emerges soak-ing wet into a comparatively chilly room. Because the newborn has a higher ratio of surface area to volume than an older infant and because it has thinner layers of fat and skin, it loses considerable body heat despite its relatively high metabolic rate.

A similar shock comes from intense light, to which the newborn is hypersensitive. There is some evidence that intense external light is visible to the fetus, which moves when such a light is applied to the mother's abdomen (Sadovsky and Polishuk 1977). However, the fetus certainly does not experience illumination comparable to that of the outside world. The immaturity of the newborn's vision, relative to other senses, may serve as a buffer. Nonetheless, exposure to constant high-intensity light—experienced by premature babies in intensive care, for example—can contribute to visual defects (Glass et al. 1985). To reduce these potential shocks from cold and light some have preferred types of delivery such as the Leboyer method. In this method the newborn is delivered into a very warm, dark, silent room and then immediately, without cutting the umbilical cord, placed against its mother's skin. Investigations of this method suggest, however, that the baby is not necessarily made more comfortable; in fact, the body temperature of the Leboyer baby is lower than that of babies handled in the more standard way (Saigel et al. 1981).

Similar claims made by the pediatricians Klaus and Kennell about the importance of immediate skin-to-skin contact with the mother led to the very important practice of "rooming-in" for babies and mothers (Klaus and Kennell 1982). Unfortunately they went on to suggest that these early moments of skin-to-skin contact were critical for mother-infant "bonding." The early bonding literature and the notion that the first minutes of contact are critical have been widely criticized (Goldberg 1983; Lamb 1982). Most mothers and babies who have no early contact (for example, because the hospital does not allow it, or because the mother has delivered by Caesarean under general anesthesia, or because the baby was adopted) become just as closely "bonded."

Nonetheless, it has been widely noted that during the first twenty-four hours of life babies are the most alert they will be for the first few months. This period of time is a wonderful opportunity for the infant and parents to become acquainted. Several researchers have noted that during these early hours parents almost instinctively engage in eye-to-eye contact, stroking, and close body contact with the newborn, which make the newborn's transition into the world more comfortable (Gewirtz et al. 1979). The role of fathers has been increasingly emphasized recently as they have entered the delivery room. Several studies suggest that the father's presence during the birth enhances his involvement with the infant and that these effects continue throughout the early months of life (Rodholm 1981).

THE FIRST TESTS

The first test in life is called the Apgar (Apgar and James 1962). Some parents record the Apgar score alongside birthweight on their infant's first report card, the birth announcement. At one and five minutes after birth a nurse or the obstetrician rates the infant's heart rate, respiratory effort, reflex irritability, muscle tone, and body color. Each of those five signs is scored 0, 1, or 2, with a higher score indicating a more favorable condition (Figure 2.1). Soon after the Apgar test the newborn may be whisked away from the parents' arms to be given an assessment of neurological reflexes, called the Dubowitz, to confirm the infant's gestational age. Still another assessment of newborns is the Brazelton Neo-

SIGN	SCORE 0	SCORE 1	SCORE 2
1. Heart rate	Absent	Below 100 beats/min.	Over 100 beats/min.
2. Breathing effort	Absent	Slow, irregular	Good, crying lustily
3. Muscle tone	Limp	Some bending of arms, legs	Active motion
4. Reflex irritability (baby's reaction when soles of feet are flicked)	No response	Cry, some motion	Vigorous cry
5. Color	Blue, pale	Pink body; blue hands and feet	Completely pink

Figure 2.1. The Apgar scoring criteria.

natal Behavior Assessment Scale (Brazelton 1973). This tests neurological reflexes and responses to animate and inanimate stimulation, such as whether the infant will turn its head in the direction of a rattle, follow the examiner's face, and respond to attempts by the examiner to console the infant.

Until this scale, which was developed in the early seventies, began to be used, many parents were unaware that newborns could see and hear. It is, of course, critical that parents understand this as they begin interacting with their infants. In turn, the infant's learning about its caregivers and its early social interactions—critical developments of the first several weeks—depend on its neonatal abilities. So parents could learn about the amazing skills of their newborns, the Brazelton scale was adapted for use by parents, referred to as the Mother's Assessment of the Behavior of her Infant (MABI). What becomes immediately apparent to parents upon administering this test is that newborns have many more skills than just seeing and hearing (Field et al. 1978).

SLEEP AND LEARNING

Most of these tests and most neonatal research are performed in the first twenty-four hours. After this period the newborn adopts a schedule of being alert for only five or ten minutes at intervals of three to four hours, around feedings (Wolff 1965). The remaining hours of the day are spent sleeping, drowsing, fussing, or crying.

Because approximately twenty of those hours are spent sleeping, and because the newborn is learning so rapidly, the newborn may be learning while asleep. Evidence for learning during sleep comes from recordings of brain activity (electroencephalograms, or EEGs), which show that activity in the cortex looks very similar whether the newborn is asleep or awake (Prechtl and O'Brien 1982; Dreyfus-Brisac 1979). In addition, responses to stimulation of the newborn during sleep suggest that the newborn is processing information. For example, changes will occur in the EEG when lights are flashed or sounds are presented. These responses are similar whether the baby is awake or asleep (Akiyama et al. 1969; Ellingson 1970; Madison et al. 1986). Another piece of evidence for learning during sleep is that the process of habituation occurs more readily when the newborn is asleep than when it is awake (Ashton 1973).

Some have speculated that newborns sleep to reduce excessive amounts of stimulation. That may explain why they sleep more during daytime hours, which are more stimulating. Infant sleep patterns change dramatically over the first several months. By three months the infant is typically sleeping through much of the night, showing EEG patterns that look more like an adult's. Around nine months the infant's distribution of sleep states begins to look more adult. For example, the newborn spends more time in active sleep (the sleep state associated with dreaming) than in quiet sleep, unlike the adult. By nine months, more time is spent in quiet sleep and less time in active sleep.

PERCEPTION

The newborn has an impressive array of perceptual skills. It can sense touch and motion, discriminate tastes and smells, and hear and see surprisingly well. The senses develop in approximately that order: tactile (touch), vestibular (motion), taste, smell, hearing, and vision. This is the same order in which sensory areas of the brain develop, and the order in which the world is experienced, first in the womb (where sensory experiences encompass all but the visual sense) and then in the outside world.

TOUCH AND MOTION

The most developed senses, the tactile and vestibular systems, are certainly exercised in the womb as the fetus performs its gymnastics. The tactile sense is the first to function, with the somatosensory cortex being the most developed at birth. The vestibular sense is the first to mature. At as early as three months' gestation the fetus will move its face towards a tactile stimulus (such

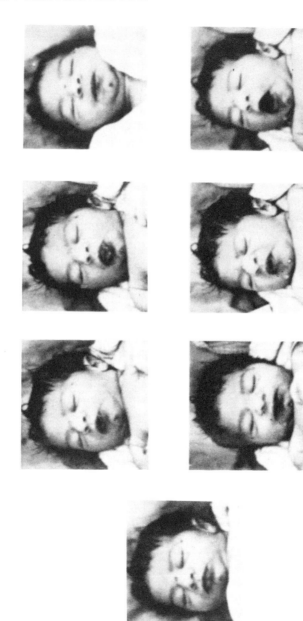

Figure 2.2. Left, newborn infant's face at rest; *top row,* response to sweet taste; *bottom row,* response to bitter taste.

as a hair). Shortly after birth the newborn can discriminate the touch of brush hairs of various diameters, and respond to electrical stimuli and puffs of air that are barely discernible by an adult (Humphrey 1972; Jacklin et al. 1981; Ellis and Ellingson 1973; Yang and Douthitt 1974). Its vestibular sense is also well developed. The newborn feels motion when carried about or rocked and will become sick if spun around too rapidly on a merry-go-round apparatus. If the newborn is spun in either direction, its eyes will move in the opposite direction to maintain a constant focus on an object. These eye movements are called nystagmus. If the newborn is held in a stationary position while objects are twirled about it, its eyes will move in a similar fashion (Hainline et al. 1984). Although the sense of balance is not yet developed, the newborn will attempt to right its head when placed in awkward positions, such as with the head flopping backward or to the side.

TASTE AND SMELL

The chemical senses, taste and smell, are also well developed in the newborn. Newborns make distinct facial expressions when they taste sweet, sour, and bitter solutions, similar to the facial expressions of adults tasting the same substances (Steiner 1979; Ganchrow et al. 1983; Rosenstein and Oster 1988). The newborn responds to sweet substances with a smile, to sour with puckered lips, and to bitter with an expression of disgust (Figure 2.2). Smiling suggests the neonate's preference for sweet solutions; the newborn also shows this preference by sucking more vigorously for sweet solutions, except when they become too sweet (Crook 1978). Parents recognize almost immediately that newborns will suck harder for milk than for water or even for sugar water, suggesting a discriminating palate. The newborn's discrimination of odors also probably plays a part in food preferences.

Newborns show very clear odor preferences and aversions. Positive facial expressions are observed when the newborn is presented with fruit odors, and disgust expressions occur with fishy and rotten-egg odors (Steiner 1979). Newborns will turn away from ammonia, but will turn toward more pleasant odors (Rieser et al. 1976). These discriminations are also noted in habituation studies, in which one odor is presented repeatedly. Respiratory and activity changes decrease with repeated presentations of one odor but reappear when a new odor is introduced. Discrimination has been shown in this way between the similar odors of anise oil and asafetida (Engen and Lipsitt 1965). In addition, a newborn repeatedly exposed to a pleasant odor (such as ginger or cherry) will prefer the familiar odor (Balogh and Porter 1986). A much more subtle discrimination is shown by the finding that newborns will orient toward the odor of their own mother's breast pads but not to an unused breast pad or one taken from an unfamiliar nursing mother (McFarlane 1975; Cernack and Porter 1985).

HEARING AND SPEECH PERCEPTION

Newborns respond to sounds of varying intensity and frequency. The Brazelton neonatal assessment tests their ability to localize sound by making a rattle sound on one side of the head and then the other and observing whether the newborn turns in its direction. The sophisticated ability to discriminate sounds was demonstrated in a study that presented buzzer and rattle sounds to sleeping newborns (Field et al. 1979). In habituation trials of repeating one stimulus, reduced limb movements and decreased heart rate were noted. When the other stimulus was introduced the newborns renewed their limb movements and heart rate responses, suggesting that they had discriminated between the rattle and the buzzer (Figure 2.3).

More interesting auditory stimuli have been used to study newborns' sound discrimination, for example, tapes of the mother's heartbeat and crying sounds of other infants. The mother's heartbeat can be used as a reinforcer of newborn activity, perhaps because of exposure to it in utero (DeCasper and Sigafoos 1983). When crying sounds of another infant are presented the newborn will continue to cry. But when the newborn's own cry sounds are presented the newborn will cease crying, suggesting that the newborn can discriminate its own from others' cry sounds (Martin and Clark 1982; Simner 1971; Sagi and Hoffman 1976). The response to the crying of others has been labeled an empathy response.

Several researchers have noted newborns' preference for the human voice and their ability to discriminate among spoken sounds. One research group found that newborns moved their limbs in synchrony with taped speech (Condon and Sander 1974). By correlating film of the newborns' behavior as they listened with the tape recordings they were hearing, it was shown that distinct limb movements corresponded to the onset of separate speech segments. Such movements did not occur in response to tapping sounds. This implies neonatal discrimination of adult speech, although other researchers have failed to replicate this phenomenon (Dowd and Tronick 1986).

It has been already noted that the newborn prefers its own mother's voice. In one study newborns were presented with audiotapes of their mothers and other mothers reading the same story (DeCasper and Fifer 1980). By varying the interval between bursts of sucking

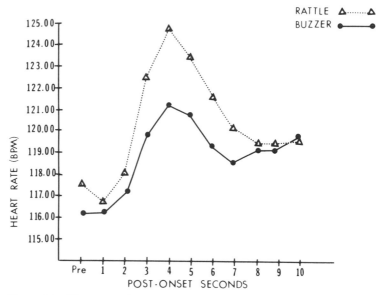

Figure 2.3. Heart rate habituation to stimulus from a rattle and a buzzer.

on a pacifier, the infants could trigger one or the other audiotape. Some newborns had to shorten the intervals and others had to lengthen them in order to produce their own mother's voice. The newborns learned to produce their own mother's voice by varying their sucking behavior, which suggests that they prefer it. This preference probably relates to in utero experience with the mother's voice.

The same research group had one group of pregnant women read aloud Dr. Seuss's "The Cat in the Hat" and another group read a version in which the words "cat" and "hat" were replaced by "dog" and "fog." After birth the newborns showed their preference for the version of the story that had been read to them in utero by learning to suck a pacifier more or less vigorously (DeCasper and Spence 1986). This suggests that newborns are capable of making very fine auditory discriminations.

VISION

One of the easiest skills to elicit in the newborn is tracking or following a visual stimulus. Most alert newborns readily perform this task during assessment with the Brazelton scale, following a brightly colored object or the face of an examiner or parent. In a more controlled investigation of this ability, moving images of normal and scrambled faces were presented to nine-minute-old newborns (Figure 2.4). The newborns turned their eyes and heads to follow the real faces across their visual field. Because this tracking ability was more reliably elicited by the real as compared to the totally scrambled face pattern, the newborn appears to prefer a real face (Goren et al. 1975; Dziurawiec and Ellis 1986).

Not only is a real face preferred, but the mother's face is discriminated and preferred within hours of birth. While mothers and fathers have no difficulty recognizing their newborn's face (even from photographs), the newborn's recognition of a mother's face was uncertain until recently (Kaitz et al. 1988; Field, Cohen, et al. 1984; Bushnell 1987). In one study the mother's face was presented to the infant through a trapdoor alternately with that of an unknown mother's face and the infant's looking time was measured. The infants looked for a longer time at their mother's face, suggesting that they preferred it even after only a few minutes of exposure. This demonstrated preference for the mother's face was further strengthened when the mother's voice was added.

Visual perceptions have been noted for other stimuli. For example, newborns have shown color preferences by visual fixations. They can discriminate red, green,

Figure 2.4 Scrambled and unscrambled face patterns.

yellow, and blue but they look longer at blue and green objects than at red ones of equivalent brightness, suggesting that they may be more sensitive to short-wavelength stimuli (Adams et al. 1986; Jones-Molfese 1977). Others have studied newborns' perception of shapes and spatial relationships. The newborn can discriminate two-dimensional drawings of a triangle, cross, circle, and square (Slater et al. 1983). Further, when shapes are moved around the newborn can perceive their different spatial arrangements (Antell and Caron 1985). Newborns can also perceive the difference between two and three dots, possibly suggesting a very early numerical ability (Antell and Keating, 1983).

Still other studies have looked at the newborn's perceptions of three-dimensional objects. Three-dimensional objects can be discriminated, as well as their hardness or softness (Slater et al. 1984; Rochat 1987). Newborns can also perceive three-dimensional space. Bower, for example, investigated whether infants perceive objects as graspable (Bower 1974). The infants wore polarizing goggles that presented the illusion of a graspable object. The infants cried when grasping at the illusion, suggesting that this is a violation of their perception. Without the goggles, the infants were presented with two objects, one within and one beyond their reach. The infants made twice as many attempts to reach the closer object. Bower and his colleagues also tried to determine whether newborns can perceive an object rotating in such a way that its forward edge appeared about to strike the baby in the face. They used a shadow-casting device, which elicited self-defensive behavior such as turning away, suggesting that the newborn can perceive looming objects, a very useful skill for life in this world.

INTERSENSORY PERCEPTION

A more complicated question is the discriminations newborns make involving more than one sensory system. One example of such a discrimination is that newborns prefer to look at a shape they have explored orally. Newborns were tactually familiarized with an odd-shaped pacifier by sucking on it. They were then presented with large-scale drawings of this pacifier and one of a different shape. The newborns clearly preferred to look at the pacifier they had just explored orally (Meltzoff and Borton 1979).

Imitation by the newborn is perhaps a more sophisticated example of intersensory perception (Figure 2.5). In one study adults modeled behaviors already in the newborn's repertoire, for example, opening the mouth, thrusting out the tongue, and moving the fingers (Meltzoff and Moore 1977). The newborns opened their mouths more often when mouth opening was being modeled and thrust out their tongues more often when that was being modeled. This imitative ability has been demonstrated in newborns in other cultures as well (Reissland 1988). Even more impressive is the newborn's ability to imitate facial expressions such as happiness, sadness, and surprise (Kaitz et al. 1988). The newborn has all the necessary muscles to perform the seven universal facial expressions (happiness, sadness, surprise, interest, disgust, fear, and anger) and has been shown spontaneously to produce these facial expressions in response to the appropriate portions of the Brazelton assessment (Field, Greenberg, et al. 1984). When a researcher modeled a series of happy faces followed by a series of sad and then surprised faces, the new-

Figure 2.5. A newborn infant imitating happy, sad, and surprised facial expressions.

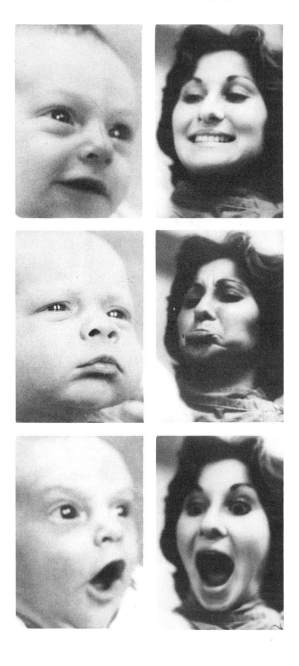

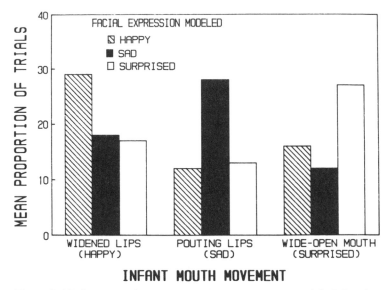

Figure 2.6 Infant mouth movement in response to modeled facial expressions.

borns were able to discriminate these facial expressions. They showed this by habituation, or reduced response to a repetition of one face and renewed response to another face (Field et al. 1982). In addition, they showed imitative abilities by widening their lips during the modeling of happy faces, protruding their lower lips during the modeling of sad faces, and opening their eyes and mouths wide during the presentation of surprised faces (Figure 2.6). An observer who was unable to see the model's face was able to guess at better than chance what expression was being modeled by looking at the newborn's facial expressions. Although the underlying process whereby the newborn learns to imitate is not understood, this is certainly one of the newborn's most impressive perceptual skills.

*   *   *

In summary, the period surrounding birth is a most exciting time for all concerned. The emerging baby, who has been accustomed to warmth and darkness, is thrust into a cold, bright, unfamiliar world. At first the newborn cries in apparent discomfort at the bombardment of stimuli, and then quickly alerts to the mother's voice, face, smell and taste. Parents instinctively soothe the newborn, who in turn rewards them with wide-eyed attention and an array of facial expressions, sometimes mimicking theirs. Fortunately, the newborn's expressions and abilities are well developed because they are critically needed in the early social interactions that commence at birth.

3/ Motor Development and Learning

Social-emotional development depends on the development of sensorimotor and cognitive skills. Some discussion of these skills is essential.

Sensorimotor development is probably the most noticeable and observable process in infancy. Motor milestones such as sitting up, manipulating objects, crawling, and walking are obvious and distinctive. Parents notice and proudly announce these milestones to the world; if they do not occur on schedule, parents express considerable concern. Motor development occurs at a rapid pace. In about a year the infant progresses from relative helplessness to being able to walk alone. Because each milestone is reached on schedule, motor development has been considered a biological maturational process. Aside from its importance for mobility, independent locomotion, and manipulation of objects, motor development is critical for facilitating perceptual, cognitive, and social-emotional development.

The impressive perceptual system of the newborn becomes considerably more differentiated and sophisticated in the months following birth. Some of this development is related to cognitive skills such as an increasing ability to process information and a developing memory. However, much of it is related to the infant's developing motor skills which enable it to manipulate objects and explore the world. These activities in turn enhance the infant's cognitive development.

Motor development appears to depend in part on the growth of the infant. The newborn on average weighs about 3500 g (8 lbs.) but is only 50 cm (20 in. long), a considerable bulk for its length. This bulk is comprised mostly of fatty tissue and very little muscle (Illingworth 1973). The newborn has a very heavy head which is also much larger in relation to its body. Its limbs are disproportionately shorter given the size of its trunk. These features make for awkward and limited mobility, compounded by disorganized limb movements and reflexive behaviors. Because of the infant's growth pattern (in which length outpaces weight), postural developments, and the disappearance of reflexes, voluntary controlled motor movements soon develop.

REFLEXES

At birth the newborn has a host of involuntary behaviors called reflexes. Darwin was one of the earliest students of neonatal reflexes. In his 1877 biographical sketch he described his son's reflexes: "During the first seven days various reflex actions, namely sneezing, hickuping, yawning, stretching and of course sucking and screaming were well performed by my infant. On the seventh day, I touched the naked sole of his foot with a bit of paper, and he jerked it away, curling at the same time his toes, like a much older child when tickled. The perfection of these reflex movements shows that the extreme imperfection of the voluntary ones is not due to the state of the muscles or the coordinating centres, but to that of the seat of the will" (Darwin 1877).

Because reflexes are automatically set off, they may

make the newborn look out of control. However, their absence elicits concern among neonatologists and pediatric neurologists. Reflexes of the face, hands, feet, and body routinely appear on neurological examinations such as the Prechtl Neurological Examination and the Brazelton Neonatal Behavioral Assessment Scale (Prechtl 1977; Brazelton 1973).

Two important reflexes of the face are rooting and sucking. Rooting is elicited simply by touching the infant's cheek; the infant will turn its mouth in the direction of the touch. If a finger is placed in its mouth it will suck on it. Another reflex is the newborn's response to a cloth or some other object placed on its face: the newborn makes swiping movements with its arms and turns it head. The value of these reflexes for the infant's survival is obvious. Another classic reflex is called the tonic neck reflex. If the head is moved to one side when the infant is lying on its back the newborn will assume a "fencing position," moving the opposite arm up to the back of its head.

The predominant reflex of the hand is called the "palmar grasp." Place your finger on the palm of the newborn's hand and its fingers will grasp and completely encircle your finger. This grasp is so tight that you can then pull the infant to a sitting or a standing position. The foot grasp, or plantar grasp, can be elicited by simply placing a finger at the base of the newborn's toes, which will result in the toes curling about the examiner's finger. Another foot reflex is called the Babinski: if you scratch the outside of the sole of the foot, the toes will fan out.

Reflexes which involve the entire body include the Moro reflex, placing, standing, and walking. The Moro reflex is elicited by allowing the baby's head to drop slightly (Figure 3.1). This is followed by a sequence of

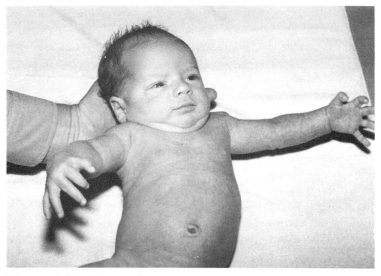

Figure 3.1. The Moro reflex.

arm extension with the hands open followed by flexion with the hands clenched. This movement is also seen in our primate relatives. A reflex that is like a precursor to later development is the crawling reflex. An infant placed in a prone position will turn its head to the side and make crawling-like movements, mostly pushing from its feet. Other reflexes that look like precursors to later development are placing, standing, and walking. If the infant is held upright under its arms it will readily place its feet as if to stand and then, particularly if held leaning slightly forward, will proceed to take steps (Figure 3.2).

Many of these reflexes disappear within a few months of birth. Some think they disappear because of lack of use or because of insufficient muscle strength as weight increases (Thelen and Fisher 1982). Others think that reflexes are suppressed as the cortical regions of the

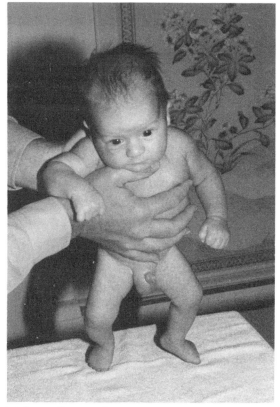

Figure 3.2. The walking reflex.

brain develop. Reflexes are thought to be controlled by the midbrain, and the cortical areas exert inhibitory control over midbrain functions. It is interesting that adults with cortical damage experience a reemergence of infant reflexes (Paulson and Gottlieb 1968).

Why these reflexes develop is yet another question. Some view reflexes as innate forms of behavior that had some adaptive value in evolution (Jersild 1955). For example, the Moro reflex could allow the infant to cling to the mother. Others consider that these reflex behaviors developed as adaptations to the fetal environment (Prechtl 1981). For instance, the walking reflex could have developed to allow the fetus to move around in the womb. Being able to move prevents the fetus from becoming fixed in one position and allows it to position itself head-down for birth (Iannirubuerto 1985).

Because many of these reflex behaviors look like precursors to later voluntary behaviors such as grasping, stepping, and walking, investigators have wondered if their exercise would lead to earlier voluntary movements. One researcher exercised the walking reflex in very young infants (Zelazo 1976). Voluntary walking developed much earlier in these infants. Although early walking may have its advantages, the investigators did not assess whether these infants experienced slower development in other areas. The normally dormant period between the early reflexes and the later voluntary behavior may be necessary for other developments, such as motor control for better voluntary walking or eye-hand coordination for more finely tuned grasping. When the timetable for motor development appears so invariant and universal, we should be reluctant to accelerate specific skills without knowing how it may affect the development of other skills.

MOTOR SKILLS

The development of sitting and walking is critical for developments in perception and cognition. Learning to sit up extends not only the infant's visual world but also its opportunities for manipulating objects. Learning to walk considerably extends the infant's exploration in space. Although there is some variability in the timing of motor milestones, the sequence appears to be invariant. An infant can lift its head in the prone position at around three weeks, lift its chest in the prone position at around two months, roll over at approximately four to five months, sit alone at around seven months, crawl at approximately eight months, stand alone somewhere between ten and twelve months, and walk alone at around one year to fourteen months. These gross motor skills are measured by the standard infant developmental assessments such as the Denver Developmental Screening Test and the Bayley Motor Scale (Bayley 1969).

Fine motor skills, such as reaching, grasping, and manipulating objects, are assessed on the Bayley Mental Scale. Newborns are capable of a form of reaching that disappears around four weeks. A different form of reaching appears around four months. Reaching involves the movement of the hand toward an object and closure of the hand on the object. Ideally the newborn's hand is open as it moves toward the object and closes on the object as contact is made. Newborns often make errors, with the hand closing sometimes before it gets to the object and sometimes well after it gets to it.

In the later form of reaching which occurs at about four months, there is a gap of about a third of a second between bringing the hand to the object and closing the hand on the object. In this case reaching and grasping are separate activities. Also, in the newborn one-handed reaching is more common and in the older infant two-handed reaching is more common. The latter is more functional because one hand can correct for an error made by the other hand. In this more developed reaching and grasping behavior there is more visual control, with the infant continually monitoring and correcting the distance between its hand and the object. Some researchers have claimed that true reaching does not occur until this later stage (Ruff and Malton 1978; Rader and Stern 1982; Von Hofsten 1984; McDonnell et al. 1983). In fact, some have referred to newborn reaching and grasping behavior as a reflex pattern because it appears automatically when an object is placed in front of a newborn. Some have preferred to call it undifferentiated behavior. Bower, who conducted many experiments on this behavior, suggests that the very young infant is perceptually as well as motorically sophisticated, but initially lacks differentiation of the senses and the motoric acts (Bower et al. 1979). He considers that the general process underlying early development is this differentiation.

Most developmental psychologists agree that early experiences are important in facilitating motor developments (such as practice with crib and playpen mobiles for developing reaching and grasping skills, or parents' assistance with walking), but still consider that the developmental milestones occur on a programmed schedule. In a classic study of identical twin girls, one girl was trained in motor tasks while the other was not (Bower 1982). Because the twins were genetically identical, their maturational rate should have been the same unless the training made a difference. The training appeared to have no effect on the development of the various motor skills, leading the author to conclude that the development of motor skills is primarily determined by maturation. However, other studies have shown slight variations in the timing of the onset of motor skills that result from environmental input. For example, a group of infants who were presented with completely rigid objects that did not move when the infant grasped them were slow in developing the more sophisticated reaching and grasping pattern. It is interesting that the two major milestones of reaching and walking are considerably delayed in blind infants, suggesting the importance of visually directed experience.

LEARNING

The infant learns to do virtually everything that is typically human during the first two years of life—to stand and walk erect, to use tools, to talk, even to perform mathematical operations such as counting. An understanding of how this comes about in so brief a time and by what processes is particularly elusive. Learning is usually defined as a change of behavior resulting from experience and practice. The infant experiences the world and practices behavior with a vengeance; diaries of infant development are replete with daily milestones in learning. Yet researchers know very little about how these come about. Even more perplexing is the process of memory. Once learned, how are these behaviors remembered? Very little long-term memory is attributed to young infants; few of us remember our own infancies. Yet, without memory, that which was learned would not be retained.

BEHAVIORIST THEORY

In the behaviorist orientation, one of the most popular approaches, learning is inferred from changes in responses to stimulation. The processes by which learning is thought to occur include habituation and various forms of conditioning.

Habituation. Habituation is considered the most primitive form of learning. The first presentation of a stimulus elicits an orienting response, characterized by quieting, attentiveness, and heart rate deceleration (Graham and Clifton 1966; Slater et al 1984). After the stimulus is repeatedly presented, the infant learns to recognize the stimulus and stops responding. If a new stimulus is presented, the orienting response occurs again. In habituation studies researchers typically present the stimulus a predetermined number of times or present it until the infant no longer responds. Then a novel stimulus is presented.

Operant conditioning. Whereas habituation is simply the weakening of an unlearned response to stimulation, operant conditioning requires the modification of an existing response. The investigator typically waits for a behavior that is already in the infant's repertoire, such as sucking, head turning, or kicking, and then reinforces that response with a positive or negative stimulus (depending on whether the investigator wants to increase or decrease the rate of the infant's behavior). The infant then learns the relationship between the behavior (the operant) and the reinforcer. Illustrations of this type of conditioning are studies where infants learned to alter their sucking rhythms to receive a sweet fluid or to hear their mothers read a story (DeCasper and Fifer 1980). Other infant responses conditioned by this procedure include leg movements or head turning to move a mobile, and sucking to produce pictures (Rovee and Rovee 1969; Watson and Ramey 1972; Siqueland and DeLucia 1969; Fagen and Ohr 1985).

Classical conditioning. In this form of conditioning, a neutral stimulus (the conditioned stimulus) is presented with a stimulus that already elicits a response in the infant (the unconditioned stimulus). For example, touching an infant's cheek (unconditioned stimulus) elicits the response of rooting or head turning (unconditioned response). If a tone (the conditioned stimulus) is sounded prior to touching the infant's cheek, it will eventually elicit head turning (the conditioned response) without the touching stimulus. In a classic experiment with newborns, tones are paired with the insertion of a nipple to condition sucking (Lipsitt and Kaye 1964; Blass et al. 1984).

Operant and classical conditioning combined. In this procedure a conditioned stimulus is associated with an unconditioned response through reinforcement. For example, in one study a tone (the conditioned stimulus) was followed by head turning (the unconditioned response), which was reinforced by giving the infant sugar water. If the head turning did not occur spontaneously after the tone was sounded, the experimenter turned the infant's head (always in one direction) and then gave the reinforcer. The experimenter then subjected this conditioned response to extinction: after the infant had responded several times to the tone by turning its head in the correct direction, the tone was presented without reinforcement until the infant made several consecutive responses of turning its head in the opposite direction. Finally, this procedure was used to train the infant to respond to a tone by turning its head in one direction, and to a buzzer by turning its head in the other direction (Blass et al. 1984).

Contingent social stimulation. One of the most effective reinforcements of operant learning is social stimulation, such as talking, touching, or presenting one's face to the infant when the infant produces the desired response. Typically, conditioning with social stimulation has been used to increase the infant's social responses. For example, increased smiling in four-month-old infants is conditioned by picking them up, talking softly to them, and patting them each time they smile (Brackbill 1958). Another use of this method is to reduce fussiness by reinforcing the infant's nonfussy vocalizations (Rheingold et al. 1959).

Although contingent social stimulation is a very effective reinforcer of behavior, it is not clear whether it is the social stimulation itself or the fact that the social stimulation is contingent on a response of the infant that makes this form of learning effective. Infants, like adults, learn more effectively when they see that their own behavior modifies the environment. In the infant's home environment there are many sources of contingent social stimulation. Most people do not respond immediately to every behavior an infant shows; however, reinforcing a response immediately after its occurrence is the most effective way of ensuring that the response will be repeated.

PIAGETIAN THEORY

A second popular approach to learning is based on the work of Jean Piaget. He traced the cognitive development of his own three children by observing and experimenting with their activities (Piaget 1952, 1954, 1962). Piaget suggested that intelligence is the ability to adapt to the environment—to act on information in the environment using skills that are already developed. When those skills are not effective in mastering the information, a child modifies its skills so that the information can be processed.

According to Piaget, infants during the sensorimotor period (birth to two years) learn by assimilation and accommodation. An infant assimilates information by applying existing skills and responses to events and experiences. Accommodation is the complementary process: the infant accommodates its behavior when the skills it already has cannot achieve a desired goal or accomplish a task. Piaget describes the infant as passing through several stages of development. The first, the reflexive stage, lasts for approximately the first month of life. During this stage the infant's reflexes are gradually modified as the infant learns voluntary behavior. Sucking and grasping are typical reflexes; modifications of these behaviors are required by different forms of feeding or different objects for grasping.

The second stage, which consists of "primary circular reactions," lasts for the next few months of life. The infant practices grasping objects and sucking on them at the same time or looking at objects and grasping them at the same time, not for the effect that its behaviors have on the objects but for the mere experience of practicing them. The third stage is that of "secondary circular reactions" and lasts from approximately four to eight months of age. While the infant in the previous stage acted for the pleasure of the action itself, in this stage the infant appears to have intentional behavior. The infant shows slight alterations in behavior or uses an object slightly differently to see what results can be produced.

The fourth stage, which lasts from approximately eight to twelve months, involves the "coordination of secondary schemes." By this stage the infant has gained the ability to identify causal relationships. Piaget gives an example: his eight-month-old catches sight of her big brother's toy, which she is unable to reach. After several attempts to reach it she pulls on the towel lying underneath the toy to bring the toy within reach. Piaget and others (such as Bruner and Vygotsky) have suggested that the use of physical tools and of symbolic tools, like language, are complementary during infancy and early childhood (Bruner 1972; Vygotsky 1978). As spoken language increases, tool use temporarily decreases (Baillargeon and Graber 1988).

During this stage infants also learn object permanence. That is, the infant will now search for hidden objects by removing the cover and then grasping the object. The infant has learned the relationship between the cover and the object and that the object continues to exist even when the cover masks it. The infant is thought to learn person permanence—that when the mother leaves the room she does not disappear forever—in much the same way. Some think this process is essential for the development of social attachments. Piaget describes his daughter Lucienne confronting the issue of person permanence at the age of fifteen months: "Lucienne is in the garden with her mother. Then I arrive; she sees me come, smiles at me, therefore obviously recognizes me (I am at a distance of about 1 meter 50). Her mother then asks her: 'Where is papa?' Curiously enough, Lucienne immediately turns toward the window of my office where she is accustomed to seeing me and points in that direction. A moment later we repeat the experiment; she has just seen me 1 meter away from her, yet, when her mother pronounces my name, Lucienne again turns toward my office.

"Here it may be clearly seen that if I do not represent two archetypes to her, at least I give rise to two distinct behavior patterns not synthesized nor exclusive of one another but merely juxtaposed: 'papa at his window' and 'papa in the garden' " (Piaget 1954).

The fifth stage, between approximately one year and eighteen months, is that of "tertiary circular reactions." Here the child is interested in the effects produced by its behavior as well as in the various properties of objects. The sixth and final stage of infancy concerns the "invention of new means through mental combinations" and lasts from approximately eighteen months to the end of infancy (twenty-four months). The child is no longer engaging in trial and error behavior but begins to see solutions to problems without having to go through the steps of experimenting. The classic example given by Piaget is that of his son, who when he could not reach an object immediately grasped a stick and drew the toy within reach. This test is now part of the Bayley developmental examination; a child of this age is expected to perform it with no difficulty.

Piaget developed his description of these stages as he observed his three children. Such observations, along with such simple experiments as he performed, whether or not they can be verified in the laboratory, are a rich source of material in infant learning. They highlight the knowledge that can be gained from simply observing and playing exploratory games with infants.

EXPLORATION AND PLAY

Infants learn mostly from exploration and play. Through these activities the infant experiences the world, comes to know and predict it. Infants clearly enjoy the opportunity to explore and play. In the first few months most exploration of the infant's environment is done through the ears, eyes, and nose. Later the infant becomes capable of reaching for, grasping, and manipulating objects. At this time virtually everything is explored by mouth. By six or seven months the infant is capable of locomotion and starts to actively explore and interact with the environment, greatly enlarging its world.

In exploration, the infant shows an intent, concentrated facial expression of interest. When responding to something new, the infant will repeat the activity it is performing several times, as if to inquire what the object does. Only when the object becomes familiar does play begin. In this activity the infant typically has a relaxed or contented facial expression. It engages in a variety of activities as if exploring what can be done with the object. At this point learning takes on the look of creativity and the infant expresses great glee, as if having recognized its mastery of the activity (Hutt 1970; Sullivan and Lewis 1988).

One of the most important facilitators of infant exploration and play is the presence of a parent. By six or seven months the infant is usually capable of locomotion and shows his autonomy by crawling away from the parent to explore the environment. At first the infant will remain within close range of the parent, but as locomotion develops and as exploratory appetite increases it moves farther away, remaining separated from the parent for longer periods of time. In a number of experiments it has become clear that when the infant is playing with the mother or father present, the infant will move away and explore the environment voluntarily (Rheingold and Eckerman 1969). However, if the parents are absent, the infant's exploration of the environment is greatly decreased.

The parents' behavior also directly affects the exploratory behavior of the infant. In one study, mothers were instructed to provide varied amounts of attentiveness to their infants for a month (Rubenstein 1967). At the end of the month the infants' exploratory behavior toward a novel stimulus (a bell) was observed. The high maternal-attentiveness infants exceeded both the medium and the low maternal-attentiveness infants in their exploratory behavior toward the novel stimulus, and in fact preferred it to a familiar stimulus. Another demonstration of the same phenomenon is that infants whose mothers respond positively to their infants' vocalizations manipulate novel toys more often than infants who do not receive these responses (Yarrow et al. 1972). Maternal encouragement and attention in infancy have also been used to predict competence in language, play, and cognition (Rubenstein 1967; Tamis-Le Monda and Bornstein 1984). Finally, infants whose parents restrict their exploration do not perform as well on infant developmental tests. These tests, for example the popular Bayley infant development scales, are made up almost exclusively of items that assess the infants' exploration and manipulation of objects. It is not surprising, therefore, that infants whose parents provide many opportunities for exploration and reinforce their infants' attempts to explore and play with objects will perform better on such tests.

MEMORY

One of the paradoxes of development is that the effects of early experiences can persist into adolescence and adulthood although the experiences are forgotten during infancy, as the deficits in infant memory suggest. We do know from recent studies that infants have short-term and even long-term memory. Indeed, newborns even appear to remember prenatal events. In one study described earlier, newborn infants appeared to remember for at least several days the stories they had been exposed to prenatally (DeCasper and Fifer 1980). Another study noted that newborns (only fifty-five hours old) could remember for six to ten hours the sounds they learned to elicit by sucking (DeCasper and Spence 1986).

Slightly later in infancy (at two to four weeks) infants who had heard speech sounds sixty times each day for thirteen days could remember these speech sounds for up to two days after the last exposure (Ungerer et al.

1978). At three months, infants remembered a mobile they had moved by kicking movements when the mobile was attached to their legs. This memory lasted as long as four weeks after the original exposure (Rovee-Collier et al. 1980). By five months infants can remember abstract patterns or photographed faces for as long as fourteen days (Fagan 1971, 1973). This long-term recognition memory not only is present in the early months of life but also is not easily disrupted. Infants remember the faces even when new photographs of faces are presented to interfere with that memory (Fagan 1977; Cohen et al. 1977). Visual recognition memory appears to be related to later cognitive functioning. When infants who were given these visual recognition memory tests early in infancy were given vocabulary tests of intelligence at four to seven years, significant relationships were reported between the early recognition memory and the later intelligence test scores (Fagan and Mc-Grath 1981; Fagan 1982).

An impressive demonstration of the persistence of infant memory was reported in a paper entitled "When they were very young: Almost-threes remember two years ago" (Myers et al. 1987). In this study infant memory persisted for as long as two years. Children who had participated several times between one and ten months of age in a study on the perception of auditory space, returned to the laboratory two years later. Several measures of the children's behavior indicated that the two-year-olds remembered sounds they had heard, as well as objects they had seen and felt in the laboratory in both light and darkness. As the authors suggest, the ability of the children to remember these events was probably facilitated by the unique context and procedures of the infant study, such as alternating periods of light and dark, luminous objects, invisible sounds, and objects revealed by a rising screen. Memories reported in more anecdotal studies also tend to be of singular events. This demonstration of long-term memory is especially interesting because the infants had no language ability when they were exposed to this stimulation but did have language ability when they were asked to remember it. Most researchers had previously thought that children could not remember events they experienced prior to the development of language.

Once again infants have surprised us. They appear not only to learn by a number of complex processes, but also to remember interesting events days, months, and even years later. Like motor development, learning and memory seem to be enhanced by social interaction.

4/ Emotions, Interactions, and Attachments

To develop socially and emotionally the infant needs human contact. Infants learn to discriminate the special properties of humans from a very early age as they experience social interactions. They show different emotions and develop social communication skills, such as listening and taking turns, during early interactions. Some have argued that the infant comes into the world a ready-made social-emotional being; in any case, development of these aspects is enhanced by experience with other people. The ability to make facial expressions; to discriminate others' expressions, faces, and voices; to interact with others; and to develop attachments or relationships are some of the skills necessary for social-emotional development.

FACIAL EXPRESSIONS

Infants come into the world able to produce the seven basic, universal facial expressions—happy, sad, surprised, interested, disgusted, angry, fearful (Oster and Ekman 1978). All of these expressions have been observed during the Brazelton Neonatal Behavior Assessment (Field et al. 1984). For example, the newborn showed an interested face when a rattle was shaken at the side of its head, a disgusted face when sucking on the examiner's soapy-tasting finger, and an angry face during some of the more uncomfortable reflex testing. In addition, happy, sad, and surprised expressions on adults' faces can be imitated by many infants. In one study on the imitation of expressions, an observer was able to guess the facial expression being modeled by looking at the face of the infant (Figure 4.1; Field et al. 1983). While these expressions occur very rarely in the newborn, they are very apparent by two to four months. In one study, infants were filmed playing with their mothers and with strangers (Emde et al. 1978). The mothers were asked to view slide and motion-picture presentations of the infants' expressions. The mothers could classify each of the infants' facial expressions as one of the universal expressions. In other studies infants have been filmed responding to a variety of situations, including inoculations, a peek-a-boo game, and the approach of a stranger (Izard et al. 1980; Hiatt et al. 1979). Without contextual information, adults were able to identify the facial expressions appropriate to each situation looking at slides or films of the infants' faces. These studies suggest that infant facial expressions can be easily recognized and classified using the same categories that are used with adults.

Infants can also discriminate among these universal facial expressions. Usually this is tested by habituation. Another demonstration is the visual preference test. A photograph of a face is presented repeatedly until the infant is familiar with it. The first photograph is then presented alongside a photograph of the face with a novel expression. If the infant shows a preference for the novel photograph, it has apparently learned the expression in the first one. Newborns can habituate to live models' happy, sad, and surprised expressions. At later

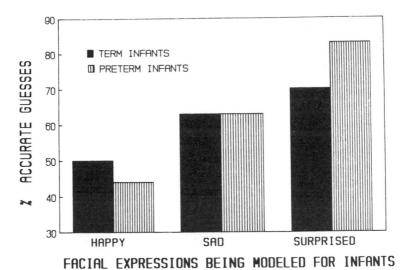

Figure 4.1. Accurate guesses of facial expressions being modeled for term and preterm infants.

ages infants can discriminate slides of joyful, angry, and neutral expressions (La Barbera et al. 1976; Haviland and Lelucia 1987; Ludemann and Nelson 1988). This suggests that live expressions may be easier to discriminate than photographed faces. In addition, there is evidence that infants can discriminate positive facial expressions better than negative or neutral facial expressions. Infants also produce positive expressions more often than negative expressions.

DISCRIMINATION OF FACES AND VOICES

Another skill that is critical to social-emotional development is the discrimination of faces and voices. This ability may be inborn. Another possible explanation is that animate faces may simply be more interesting than other visual stimuli. It is obviously useful for the infant to recognize its mother's face and voice as a newborn (Field et al. 1983; DeCasper and Fifer 1980; Sai and Bushness 1988).

The face and voice together may be even more interesting to the young infant than the face or voice alone. The newborn can follow (or track) a talking face better than the face or voice alone during the Brazelton newborn assessment. Infants at three weeks show disturbed responses if the mother's voice comes from a different direction than her face (Aronson and Rosenbloom 1971). In this study mothers were positioned face-to-face with their infants, who were behind a transparent soundproof screen. The mother's voice was presented to the infants through loudspeakers that shifted the location of the voice away from the mother's face. The infants' disturbed response suggests that the face and voice are perceived as an integrated unit.

In another study the mother's face was discriminated from a mannequin's face and an abstract facial form (a kitchen colander bent to an oval shape and painted flesh color with three colored knobs attached to create features) (Carpenter et al. 1970). Surprisingly, the infants (who ranged in age from one to eight weeks) looked at their mothers' face less than at the other objects. The investigators suggested that possibly the infants were avoiding the mother's face because she was silent rather than talkative, as the infants expected.

Infants as young as four weeks show different behaviors when positioned face-to-face with different people (Fogel 1980). In one study infants fixably stared and moved their heads in a jerky manner in the presence of an infant peer, and showed more brow movements and smooth limb movements when face-to-face with the mother. Slightly older (four-month-old) infants can discriminate reflections of themselves from others, even identical twins. They showed more gazing at their own mirror image but more smiling, vocalizing, and reaching toward twin siblings (Field 1979a). Four-month-old infants respond differently to a "talking," head-nodding, infant-size Raggedy Ann doll than to their animated mothers (Figure 4.2). They show more gazing at the doll but more social behavior toward their mothers (Figure 4.3; Field 1979d; Legerstee et al. 1987). Finally, the young infant can clearly discriminate the face and voice of their mothers from those of their fathers. Infants smile and laugh more at their fathers and gaze more at their mothers (Field 1981). These faces and voices differ on a number of dimensions such as frequency, intensity, and responsivity; the infants' responses suggest that they can discriminate very complex stimuli.

Even more impressive are infants' discriminations of subtle changes in the face and voice of the same person. Dramatic differences are noted in the infant's behavior when a mother is asked in the middle of a spontaneous interaction to look different—for example, to become silent, still-faced, joyful, or depressed (Tronick et al. 1978; Termine and Izard 1988; Gusella et al. 1988). Similarly, when the mother continues to look at the infant but changes her voice as if she were speaking to an adult (as will happen when a mirror reflection of an adult's face replaces her infant's), the infant's behavior also changes, as if the infant is aware that the mother is no longer talking to it (Trevarthen 1974). Finally, as the mother changes from being spontaneous to following instructions to be "imitative of her infant's behaviors" or to "keep her infant's attention," her infant's gaze and facial expressions change dramatically (Field 1977a). Subtle or not-so-subtle changes of face and voice, either because the interaction partners have been changed or

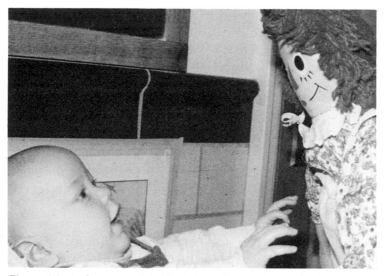

Figure 4.2. A three-month-old's interaction with an inanimate social stimulus.

because the same interaction partner is behaving differently, elicit dramatic reactions from the infant. Changes in facial expressions and heart rate suggest that the infant can discriminate the different faces and voices. This ability is most obvious when the infant is interacting with parents.

INTERACTIONS

Some investigators of early interactions have proposed that the infant is born with a very abstract awareness of the "humanness" of others plus some very general strategies for signaling that awareness to them. Many of the infant's social signals are developed during early social interactions. Infant social development is often studied through these interactions.

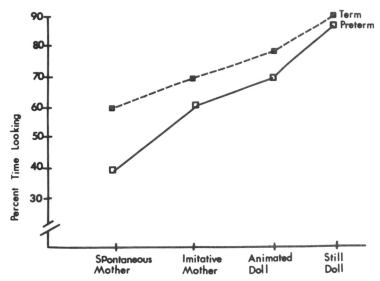

Figure 4.3. Percent of time that term and preterm infants spent looking at animate and inanimate social stimuli.

Literally dozens of early interaction studies have focused on the mother-infant pair in various contexts (feeding, face-to-face interactions, or floorplay). The parents are usually given an agenda of natural or instructed interactions. Feeding interactions are usually studied during the first few weeks, face-to-face play during the early months, and floorplay or teaching interactions during the later months, as the infants' interests and abilities shift (Field 1977a; Kaye 1977; Brazelton et al. 1974; Stern 1974; Goldberg et al. 1980). Interactions are usually spontaneous, although some have manipulated interactions by instructing the mother, for example, to remain still-faced, or to keep her infant's attention, or to imitate her infant's behavior (Field 1977a; Fogel et al. 1981). Some of these manipulations disrupt the infant's interaction behavior (for example, when the mother is still-faced, attention-getting, and depressed); others (such as the mother's joyous face and her imitations of the infant) help make the infant happier and more attentive.

Interactions are studied by being videotaped or filmed, in the home or in a laboratory. The behaviors that are assigned codes from the videotapes or from the live observations typically include gaze, vocalizations, body movements, and facial expressions. Although some have suggested that the home is a more natural setting for interactions, others have noted that the mother may feel more "on stage" in her own home. Mothers have reported feeling less nervous in the presence of a camera than of a live observer. However, knowing that they were being videotaped contributed to significant increases in talking and playful behavior (Field and Ignatoff 1981).

In many of these studies the types and amounts of behavior varied by infant age, sex, birth order, or condition (normal or at risk) and by maternal age, education, income, or cultural group. For example, depending on their age and sex infants behave differently during interactions with their mothers (Tronick et al. 1990). And volumes have been written on the ways parents from different cultures behave in interactions with their infants (Field et al. 1981; Tronick and Cohen 1989; Sostek et al. 1981; Fogel et al. 1988; Sigman et al. 1988; Roe et al. 1988). From these cross-cultural comparisons we have learned that many interaction behaviors are universal—such as baby talk, facial expressions, and infant games—but others are not. Face-to-face talk and eye contact, for example, are taboo in some cultures (Figure 4.4).

In most cultures, however, mothers behave in similarly unique ways with their infants: exaggerating facial

Figure 4.4. Infant and caregiver on the island of Ua Pou, in the Marquesas Islands (South Pacific).

and vocal expressions (as in baby talk), repeating those expressions, and imitating infant behaviors. Some have called mothers' behavior "infantized," and consider it to be pre-wired in the mother. Yet fathers, while typically more playful with their infants, behave much like mothers. This is especially true of primary caregiver fathers, whose amount of experience with their infants is similar to that of caregiver mothers and more than that of secondary caregiver fathers (Parke and O'Leary 1975; Yogman et al. 1976; Field 1978; Nimio and Rinott 1988).

Infants have also been studied interacting with their siblings and peers (Lamb 1978; Fogel 1979). One study compared infants' interactions with mother, father, siblings, and infant peers. Each of the infants' partners behaved very differently, and the infants in turn behaved differently with each partner (Field 1981). Another group showed infants mirror images of themselves on a video monitor. In one situation the videotaped infants were shown looking at the camera and in the other they were not. The infants looked at the eye-contact playback as if discovering the contingency of their own behavior. In a similar study, infants were seated face-to-face with a mirror and an infant peer. Although the infants looked more at the mirror, they showed more social behaviors with their peers (Field 1979c).

The use of multiple interaction partners leads to even more complicated results. In the presence of both peers and mothers, infants smiled and looked more at their peers and reached toward and touched their mothers more. When mothers were absent there were fewer negative behaviors toward peers than when they were present (Lewis et al. 1975; Field 1979c).

SIGNALS OF SOCIAL INTERACTION

The basic signals of social interaction are looking and talking. Because the infant's language skills are relatively unsophisticated the infant is primarily a nonverbal partner in conversation. Thus most infant-adult interaction studies have focused on infants' visual behavior, facial expressions, and body gestures. During the first few months of life, visual behavior—looking at, looking away, eye closing, and head turning—are the primary motor actions over which the infant has substantial voluntary control, and vision is the only perceptual system that can be turned on or off. At the neonatal stage, the ability to focus on and follow the human face is assessed on the Brazelton scale. Infants who demonstrate minimal alertness, cuddliness, consolability, and visual attentiveness to the adult's face and voice have been described as "difficult" babies by both researchers and the infants' mothers. Such neonatal behaviors are highly correlated with later assessments of infant temperament made by parents and by researchers (Field et al. 1978; Sostek and Anders 1977). In addition, these newborn behaviors are related to the amount of eye contact in the infants' interactions with their mothers a few months later.

Although parents almost always look at their infants, the infant's return of the gaze depends on its alertness and the parent's stimulation. The infant seems to look away from the parent's face when under- or over-aroused. Parents who are "overstimulating" and insensitive to their infant's gaze aversions are less able to hold their infant's attention; one of the most important rules for the parent to learn is that the infant occasionally needs to take breaks during the conversation. Some infants, in spite of sensitive parents, develop gaze aversion as early as at two weeks. The persistence of gaze aversion is one of the most characteristic behaviors of autistic children (Stechler and Carpenter 1967; Hutt and Dunstead 1966). Especially in our own culture, eye contact is considered an important feature of infant, child, and adult interactions.

Less frequently studied behaviors during interactions include vocalizations, facial expressions, and body gestures. Infants have been observed waving their hands at the beginning of interactions as if greeting their partner (Trevarthen 1985). A close analysis of infant interaction with speaking adults also reveals pre-speech mouth movements which approximate the vowel and consonant speech movements of the adults (Fernald and Simon 1984). Infant smiling and laughter rarely occur, except when the parent is tickling or playing a game with the infant (Sroufe and Wunsch 1972). A more common expression is the raised eyebrow, an inquisitive expression which often appears when the mother has been asked to remain still-faced.

The infant's pouting and crying faces are also familiar expressions, which usually mean discontent and the end of an interaction. Crying, arching of the back, and general squirming also typically announce the end of an interaction.

Much of the adult's activity in these interactions has been described as "infantized" behavior. Speech is slowed down and exaggerated, and the range of pitch is expanded (Fernald and Simon 1984). A study of baby talk in six languages suggested that adults vary loudness, pitch contour, rhythms, and emphasis; vowels are particularly elongated. Parents appear to slow their speech to match the infant's perceptual abilities. They also repeat themselves frequently. Facial expressions are likewise exaggerated, slowed down in their formation, and prolonged in their duration. The slowed tempo and exaggeration may enable the infant more easily to comprehend the parent's behaviors. Parents also imitate their infants to help their infants follow their behavior.

The parent's interaction repertoire also contains a number of games that appear with such frequency and universality that they might be labeled infant games. Popular games during the first months include peek-a-boo, "I'm going to get you," "tell me a story," itsy-bitsy spider, and pat-a-cake (Field 1979b). These games elicit smiling and laughter from infants at certain ages (Figure 4.5). When a mother plays age-inappropriate games—for example, pat-a-cake at six weeks instead of at twelve weeks—the interaction is disrupted.

The adult's interaction repertoire is in some ways designed especially for infants and the infant's repertoire features several behaviors that are precursors of adult behaviors. Some have speculated that the "infantized" behavior of the adult and the adult-like behavior of the

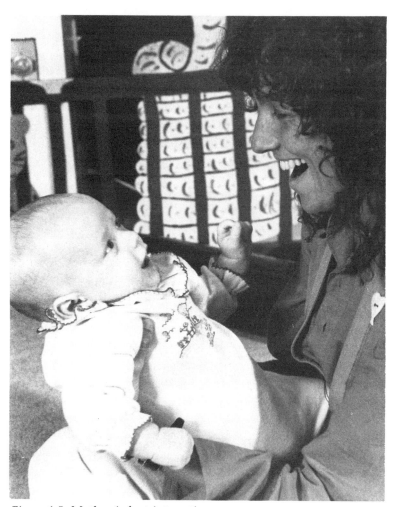

Figure 4.5. Mother-infant interaction.

infant tend to make them responsive to each other. A number of researchers have suggested that each partner in the interaction must feel that he or she has some influence on it (Lewis and Goldberg 1969; Watson 1967). If the adult's response is appropriate and occurs within a few seconds of the infant's behavior, it is more likely to be perceived by the infant as a direct response to his or her own behavior. Many of the infants' behaviors such as smiling, cooing, and eye contact are viewed by adults as responses to their own behavior and encourage the adult to play more of the same game. For example, parents often imitate their infants. Parents learn that infants both enjoy being imitated and are more able to imitate parents' imitations of their own behaviors. Thus, in early interactions there are many sequences of an infant's behavior followed by a parent's imitation, much like a game. Parents appear to enjoy being imitated by their infants (Figure 4.6).

In a similar way parents "highlight" infants' behaviors. Mothers and fathers frequently give a running commentary on or verbally describe and label their infants' behaviors as they happen—"Oh, you've got the hiccups" or "Poor baby, you always spit up when you get happy." In the game called "tell me a story" words are provided by the parent, who treats the infants' vocalizations as if they too were words: The adult asks, "Do you want to tell me a story?" The infant coos, and the adult responds, "Oh yeah? And then what happened?" The infant coos again and the adult replies "Oh, that's funny." The game continues until it no longer interests the infant, at which point the parent moves on to another game or conversation. In these conversations the infant shows relatively sophisticated, adult-like behaviors such as listening to

Figure 4.6. Mother imitating infant imitating mother.

the parent, responding with similar behaviors, and taking turns.

INDIVIDUAL DIFFERENCES IN SOCIAL SKILLS

Infants have individual differences in emotional responsivity and temperament from birth. These differences may derive from variations in genetic background and in prenatal and perinatal experiences. Some infants seem to be extremely expressive, while others are "deadpan." The expressive infants have been called "externalizers" and the nonexpressive infants "internalizers" (Field and Walden 1982; Achenbach 1980; Bates et al. 1985). This personality characteristic is thought to continue into childhood and adulthood. These individual differences have been noted as early as birth in the facial expressions infants make in response to various tastes and smells (Fox 1985). They have also been observed during neonatal assessments and facial-imitation studies. The infants at one extreme seem to be "poker-faced" but physiologically reactive to social stimulation (internalizers) and those at the other extreme are facially expressive but physiologically nonreactive (externalizers). The predisposition to be more reactive behaviorally or physiologically may have genetic origins; identical twins are more similar in these qualities than are non-identical twins (Field et al. 1982).

Individual differences in emotional responses may also be related to prenatal experiences. Different activity and reactivity levels during the fetal stage (observed through ultrasound) and emotional reactivity during the neonatal stage have been reported for those infants whose mothers experienced anxiety or depression during pregnancy (Field et al. 1985). Individual differences have also been reported for infants with congenital disorders such as Down syndrome and craniofacial anomalies, and infants with perinatal complications such as prematurity and respiratory distress syndrome (Jones 1980; Field and Vega-Lahr 1984; Lester et al. 1985). Infants experiencing these complications appear to be less active and less responsive in several ways, including facial expressions during newborn assessments and imitative expressions.

Infants also have different temperaments. Temperament is one of those few developmental phenomena that appear to be stable (Plomin 1982; Rothbart and Derryberry 1981; Kerner et al. 1985; Matheny et al. 1985; Riese 1987). Parents commonly claim that their children have been the same since birth. Parents' and researchers' ratings of temperament appear to be fairly stable and in close agreement. Consistency of temperament has also been noted during laboratory tasks, test-taking, and early interactions. In one study infant temperament was similar at three, six, and nine months, during mother-infant feeding, bathing, dressing, and play interactions in the home (Rothbart 1986). The aspects of behavior studied included activity level, smiling and laughing, fear, distress when frustrated, vocal activity, and reactivity. A similar study addressed the stability of infant temperament from three to twenty months (Field et al. 1987). The temperament dimensions of activity, rhythmicity, intensity, mood, and persistence were stable, as were the infant play interaction behaviors of looking, smiling, and vocalizing. Easier-temperament infants vocalized more and cried less frequently during play interactions.

STRANGER FEAR AND MATERNAL ATTACHMENT

Experiences critical to social-emotional development are fear of strangers and attachment to the mother (or primary caregiver), and so mothers and strangers play key roles in studies of social-emotional development. Although infants can discriminate mothers from strangers as early as at birth, they do not react negatively to strangers until they are approximately nine months old (Bronson 1972; Petrovich et al. 1989; Gewirtz and Palaez-Nogueras 1989). These negative reactions vary according to the age and appearance of the stranger; unfamiliar infants or dwarf adults are less disturbing, and a loud, rapidly approaching stranger is more disturbing (Brooks and Lewis 1976; Morgan 1973).

The infant's distress response to strangers is one indication of attachment to the mother. Another measure is the infant's behavior in the "strange situation" (Ainsworth and Wittig 1969). This research procedure begins with the mother and infant together in an unfamiliar room provided with toys and proceeds through a series of situations, each lasting about three minutes. First a female stranger joins the pair; then the mother leaves the infant with the stranger; then the mother returns. Next the mother leaves the infant alone, and after a brief interval the stranger returns. Finally the mother returns. The infant is classified according to its response to the two instances of the mother's return. Infants who greet their mothers with a smile or by showing a toy, or who approach the mother to seek comfort, are securely attached (type B). Those who fail to greet the mother (by averting their gaze) or start to approach the mother but then turn away are considered anxious/ avoidant (type A). Those who seek contact but cannot be comforted by the mother and who cry in an angry manner or hit away toys offered by the mother are considered anxious/resistant (type C). Another type, D, disorganized/disoriented, has recently been added to the classification system.

Securely attached infants typically have mothers who are more sensitive to their infants' cues, more responsive during early face-to-face interactions, and more affectionate than mothers of insecurely attached infants (Field 1987; Blehar et al. 1977; Londerville and Main 1981; Donovan and Leavitt 1989). The infants' own characteristics, such as temperament, can also influence their behavior in the strange situation (Goldsmith et al. 1986; Landau 1989). Attachment disorders occur more often in preterm infants, neglected and abused infants, and infants of alcohol-consuming or depressed mothers (Achenbach 1980; Bates et al. 1985).

Several investigators have questioned the validity of

the strange situation. The very brief separations and encounters with strangers are somewhat unrealistic. Although infants are sometimes left alone with strangers (for example, baby-sitters) and mothers may sometimes be absent for periods of time, infants rarely experience separations and encounters with strangers as brief as three minutes or repeated separations with stranger encounters over short periods of time. Infants may occasionally experience situations like the strange situation, in a day-care center for example. And those infants may learn to deal with repeated separations by avoidance or resistance. They would be classified as unattached, yet they probably are just as attached to their mothers as other infants.

Another unnatural characteristic of the strange situation is that the mothers are requested not to talk to their infants unless it is necessary. This, combined with leaving the infant alone in an unfamiliar place for brief intervals, must be stressful for some mothers and that stress is undoubtedly felt by the infants. Attachment would be better studied in nonstressful situations, with classifications based on the way the mother and infant relate to each other when they are together and not stressed.

SOCIAL REFERENCING

Another way infants tell us they are attached is their behavior when they are hurt, distressed, or needing reassurance. A securely attached infant invariably turns to the mother if she is present for comforting and reassurance. Another demonstration of the infant's attachment is the way infants refer to the mother to determine how they should react emotionally or how they should explore novel situations. This behavior is called "social referencing." The infant uses information from others' faces or voices to appraise events—for example, to determine whether a novel toy is safe (Campos and Stenberg 1981; Walden and Ogan 1988). If the mother smiles the infant is likely to approach the toy, but if the mother looks fearful the infant typically avoids the toy (Sorce et al. 1985). Infants with different temperaments respond differently to a novel situation (Feinman and Lewis 1982). In one study infants were observed encountering a caged rabbit with their mothers present (Hornik and Gunnar 1988). Wary infants were more likely to look toward their mothers when the rabbit was first presented. However, as the exploration period progressed, bold and wary infants looked at their mothers equally often. Through their facial expressions and tone of voice, as well as the content of what they said, the mothers indicated to the infants how they should respond to the situation.

SEPARATION STRESS

Another way that attachment has been measured is in long-term separations. Infants who were orphaned, hospitalized, or placed in residential nurseries during World War II commonly showed a predictable sequence of behaviors during these separations from their parents. Bowlby labelled these phases protest, despair, and

Figure 4.7. Changes in infant behavior associated with separation from the mother: (*a*) mean activity level and (*b*) heart rate in beats per minute before, during, and after the mother's hospitalizations; (*c*) infants' night wakings and crying times and (*d*) total sleep time and duration of deep sleep (B, baseline; S, separation; R, reunion).

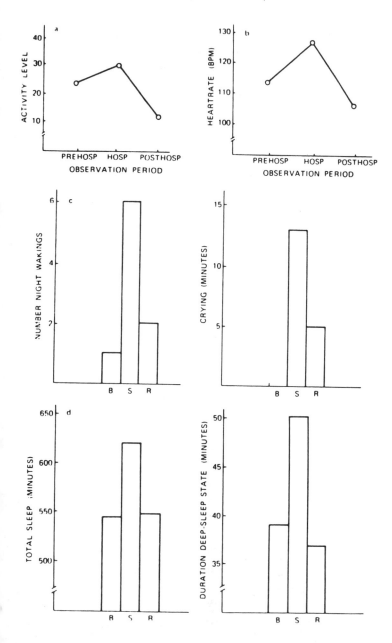

detachment (Bowlby 1969; Spitz 1946; Robertson and Robertson 1971). Protest, the initial phase, began almost immediately and lasted a few hours to a week or more. The infant appeared acutely distressed, crying loudly, throwing itself about, and looking eagerly toward any sight or sound "which might prove to be his missing mother." During the subsequent phase of despair, the infant's behavior suggested an increase in feelings of helplessness. Physical movements diminished, crying was intermittent, and the infant was withdrawn. During the next phase, detachment, the infant no longer rejected the nurses and even smiled and seemed sociable. However, when the infant's mother returned, instead of greeting her, the infant remained remote and apathetic; instead of tears there was a listless turning away, as if the infant had lost all interest in her.

In one study on more temporary forms of separation, infants were extremely agitated when their mothers were hospitalized for the birth of another child (Field 1986). After the mother returned from the hospital the infants became depressed. Before, during, and after the mothers' hospitalization the infants were videotaped during playtime and at night, and their activity level and heart rate were recorded. The parents also completed questionnaires on their infants' behaviors. During the mother's hospitalization there were increases in fussiness, activity level, heart rate, night wakings, and nighttime crying. Following the mother's return from the hospital, decreases were noted in positive affect, activity level, heart rate, and sleep, suggestive of depression (Figure 4.7). The parents also noted a number of changes including clinging and aggressive behaviors, changes in eating and toilet behavior, and sleep disturbances and illnesses. The infants were clearly agitated by this separation from their mothers, even though they visited them at the hospital during this period and were cared for by their fathers. This is certainly one of the more dramatic demonstrations of attachment to a primary caregiver.

5/ Peer Interactions and Daycare

As increasing numbers of children under the age of two years attend nursery and daycare programs, their peers are becoming important figures in their early social development. Peer interaction has become a popular research topic. Until recently very little attention was paid to infant-peer interactions, possibly because of the prevailing psychoanalytic view that the mother is the primary attachment figure during infancy. However, the observation of infants together in daycare has shown us that they are sociable with their peers from a very early age.

PEER INTERACTIONS

PEERS VERSUS PARENTS

Infant-peer interactions are studied in the same way as mother-infant interactions, typically videotaped in a laboratory setting and coded for social behaviors. Young infant pairs are considered socially interactive if they engage in face-to-face behaviors such as looking, smiling, vocalizing, and laughing. Comparisons between infants' interactions with mothers and with peers during the first few months in life suggest that infants relate very similarly to both (Field 1981; Fogel 1980). But later in the first year when infants have learned to manipulate objects and to navigate, they become more toy-directed and less interested in socializing with mothers or peers. They are considered sociable if they touch their peers, offer and accept toys, coordinate their toy play, and imitate their peers.

Basically, both peers and mothers are treated as social objects, not as toys. Because parents are more predictable and responsive than peers, interactions with them may look smoother and more sociable than with peers, who are less predictable and may challenge and frustrate each other.

In one study, behaviors of three-month-old infants were recorded when the infant was face-to-face with its mother or with a stranger peer, and when the infant was alone. The infants were sociable during both mother and peer interactions. Behavior toward the peer included intense staring and occasional straining forward of the head (apparently to get a closer look at the other infant). In the mother's presence behaviors were smoother and smiling occurred more often.

PEERS VERSUS OBJECTS

Another study illustrates the differences in infants' behavior with peers and with objects (Field 1979a). A peer and a mirror were presented sequentially and then simultaneously to three-month-old infants. The mirror image of the infant was similar in size to the live infant peer. Infants looked longer at the mirror, but smiled, vocalized, reached, and squirmed more in the presence of an infant peer. In addition, heart rate was elevated during the peer situation, probably because the infant was more aroused by the peer. The more sociable behavior directed to the peers suggests that the infant is aware of the greater potential for social interaction with another infant than with a mirror image of itself. Another study replicated these findings with infant identical twins (Field and Roopnarine 1982). There was more social behavior (smiling, vocalizing, and reaching) between the twins than between the unfamiliar infants of the earlier study. This suggests that acquaintance with peers results in even more sociability.

The next study added an infant-sized Raggedy Ann doll (Field 1981). The infant spent more time looking at the mirror, the doll, and the mother than at the peer. This gaze aversion may have occurred because the peer is a live stimulus and unpredictable. Although the mother is also a live stimulus, her behavior is more familiar and predictable. The peer may be a more arousing stimulus because of unpredictability and arousal may lead to gaze aversion. Although the infants smiled and vocalized less at the peer than at the mother, they were more sociable with the peer than with the mirror image or the doll.

These studies suggest that infants are social toward their peers from a very early age. When given an opportunity, they interact as sociably with peers as with parents. Interactions with adults do not seem to be a necessary foundation for interactions with peers. The very young infant smiles and coos at both parents and peers; older infants are less social with both, perhaps because activities with toys have become more interesting (Vandell et al. 1980).

In at least one study the presence of toys reduced the attention infants paid to mothers and peers (Eckerman et al. 1975). The mother's presence can also reduce the attention directed toward peers. In a cooperative nursery school setting, where mothers came in and out of the nursery room, infants' social

behaviors when the mother was present were compared to those when she was absent (Field 1979b).
When the infants' mothers were in the room, they vocalized more to their mothers than to their peers. They
also moved toward her, touched her, and offered her
toys more often than they did to their peers. However,
they spent more time smiling at their peers, and
equivalent amounts of time looking at their peers and
their mothers. When the infants' mothers were out of
the room, they showed fewer negative behaviors such
as taking toys from their peers and crying.

Thus mothers and toys appear to be strong competi-
tors for peer-directed behaviors. Another competitor is
the infant's drive to develop. During a motor milestone
stage—for example, the onset of walking—social behaviors appear less frequent, probably because the infant is
so busy practicing walking. Infants who are the most
mobile are the least social and verbal with each other
and, conversely, infants who cannot yet crawl or walk
exhibit the greatest number of smiles and vocalizations.
However, an increase in cognitive skills and attention
over the second year may help the infant to integrate
peer play and independent activity. Smiling and vocalizing at others are prominent early behaviors, but other
forms of social interaction require the child's integration
of activities with things and people. In addition to the
influence of competitive sources of stimulation such as
mothers and toys, infant-peer play appears to be affected by familiarity.

FAMILIARITY

Familiarity fosters behavior such as touching, hugging, and kissing. Mothers are more frequently hugged
and kissed, as are familiar peers. In one study, for example, sixteen-month-old infants who had four months

of nursery school showed more of these behaviors and more sustained interactions with their familiar peers than did sixteen-month-olds who had no nursery school experience (Mueller and Brenner 1977). To determine whether it was familiarity or nursery school experience that made the difference, infants were studied with their familiar peers and with unfamiliar infants who had also had nursery school experience (Lewis et al. 1975; Young and Lewis 1979). More body contact and touching occurred between acquaintances than between strangers. Imitative behaviors and smiling were also more frequent among acquaintances. Thus, familiarity with a particular infant appeared to facilitate social behaviors more than general experience with peers.

Other factors that affect social behavior with peers include the location of play and the diversity of toys. For example, interactions in an infant's own home typically feature more peer-directed behaviors than in someone else's home. In addition, more social behaviors are noted in floorplay with a number of toys than in playpen play with a limited number of toys.

Although increasing numbers of infants and toddlers are attending daycare or family care, very few peer studies have been conducted in those settings. One of these studies observed nursery school infants interacting with their peers during free play at the beginning and end of a semester (Roopnarine and Field 1983). Behaviors of the infants and toddlers alike changed dramatically over the semester. They looked and smiled at their peers, and approached and made physical contact with them, more often. This change during the semester was more significant than differences among age groups: the change in behavior of the youngest infants was very similar to that of the toddlers fifteen months older. Familiarity with peers seems to have a more dramatic effect on interaction behavior than developmental changes.

In summary, the small but growing literature on infant-peer interactions suggests that infants are sociable with their peers from a very early age. There are more similarities than differences between infant-parent and infant-peer interactions, particularly when contrasted with the ways infants relate to objects. The infants' peer interactions are affected by previous experiences with peers, familiarity, the presence of the mother, and the presence of toys. Comparisons of very early infant-parent and infant-peer interactions suggest that sociability with parents and peers may develop in parallel when infants have opportunities for interacting with their peers. In nursery schools where infants and toddlers have had considerable experience playing with each other, they appear to be even more sociable.

DAYCARE

A prominent psychologist recently claimed in a *Time* magazine interview that "entry into care in the first year of life is a single 'risk factor' for the development of insecure-avoidant attachment in infancy, and heightened aggressiveness, non-compliance and withdrawal in the preschool and early years" (Belsky 1987). This suggests that infant daycare may produce negative effects in two significant areas, attachment to the mother and preschool social adjustment. There are several major problems with this statement. The first is that it is based on data from low-quality daycare centers. Another is that some of the results (assertiveness and lesser compliance on the part of preschoolers with infant daycare experience) are not necessarily negative. In addition, the measurements of attachments, as I have discussed, are made in a situation that involves unnatural leavetakings and reappearances for brief periods by the mother and a stranger (Rutter 1981).

For a child who is cared for exclusively by the mother, avoidance upon the mother's return may be a pathological response to a rejecting mother. For children in daycare, however, ignoring the mother upon reunion may be an adaptive response to repeated daily separations from the mother. Greater physical distance from the mother may, in fact, signal a precocious independence. As one investigator suggested, "Is it not possible that in a child who is confident that his or her mother will return after a brief absence, the mother's return does not call for any special recognition of this event?'" (Chess 1987). There is also no reason to expect faulty attachment when children are cared for by other adults and in the company of their peers. Observations of the Efe pygmies of Zaire, where children have several adult and child caregivers, suggest that the infants have secure attachments to their mothers (Tronick et al. 1990). Further, research conducted in the Israeli kibbutz, where children are in daycare-like settings continuously from very early infancy, indicates that their attachment to their parents is quite normal (Oppenheim et al. 1988).

The second claim by Belsky, that "infants experiencing daycare in the first year are deleteriously affected in the area of early social interactions with peers and adults," is based on negative effects found in a limited number of studies. For example, in one study preschool children who had participated in infant daycare were more physically and verbally aggressive with adults and peers, less cooperative with grown-ups, and less tolerant of frustration (Schwartz et al. 1974). In another study less compliance, less persistence in dealing with difficult problems, and more negative affect were noted in infants, but the effects did not persist beyond two years of age (Farber and Egeland 1982). Decreased compliance and temper tantrums have also been noted in infants who had received outside care in their first year of life (Rubenstein et al. 1981).

In contrast, however, other studies have shown positive outcomes for infants attending daycare during their first year (Phillips et al. 1987). For example, in one study children who entered daycare as infants and had few daycare changes engaged in high levels of play with objects (Howes 1988). In another study, school-age children with extensive daycare experience did less hitting, kicking, and pushing (Haskins 1985). Children who attended daycare at an early age (between two and twenty months) laughed and touched others more often (Schwartz et al. 1973). Thus, the data on daycare experiences seem to be mixed (Zigler and Hall 1988).

Some apparent reasons for the inconsistent data are that daycare centers vary in quality, infants often have unstable daycare, and many of the infants studied come from low income families. The optimal study would be to compare infants who received quality daycare with those who were denied the same daycare because they were on a waiting list. A study of this kind compared preschool children who had received varying amounts of infant daycare (Field et al. 1988). Whether daycare began before six months of age or after six months did not have any effect on attachment to the mother or on play and socialization skills as measured by playground observations and teacher/parent behavior ratings. However, children who experienced more daycare (more hours per week over more months) were more sociable; they engaged in less watching, solitary play, and comfort-seeking behavior, and they showed more cooperative play, positive affect, peer interaction, and positive verbal interaction.

This study indicates that continuous infant daycare in quality care centers does not negatively affect attachment behavior. The same psychologist quoted in *Time* claimed in another publication that spending "more than 20 hours a week in non-maternal care during the first year of life" is a high risk factor (Belsky 1986). This statement is also contrary to the data from the study described above. Children who had received forty hours of infant daycare per week were more, not less, sociable at the preschool stage than children who attended daycare with their mothers a couple hours per week. There is no reason to expect that the daycare experience contributes to heightened aggressiveness, non-compliance, and withdrawal in the preschool years. Instead, because daycare involves extensive experience with other children and adults, it is considered a socializing experience. Indeed, by the end of grade school the children with more daycare experience in quality centers were more affectionate, assertive, and popular and less aggressive with their peers. In addition, they were more likely to be assigned to the gifted program and their math grades were higher (Field 1990).

The critical factors are the continuity and quality of care. The children who benefited from daycare attended infant daycare continuously in high quality model programs. There are still many unanswered questions regarding the risks and benefits of daycare. We need to evaluate the effects of all kinds of infant care, not just daycare (Barglow 1987).

LEAVETAKING AND ADJUSTMENT

The daily separations or leavetaking for children attending daycare can be quite stressful at first. One of the few studies on this subject took place in England (Blurton-Jones and Leach 1972). Children and parents had different leavetaking or departure styles. Some children had difficulty leaving their parents in the morning and leaving their classmates in the afternoon, suggesting general difficulty with transitions. Fussy children often had mothers who hovered around the child and then slipped out of the room. In a similar study infants were more distressed when their parents hovered about them and then sneaked out of the room (Field et al. 1984). Children who were dropped off by their mothers were more demanding and fussy than those brought by their fathers. Mothers typically hovered longer than fathers.

Other differences related to the infant's age and sex. During the first semester the toddlers (fifteen to twenty-four months) were the most distressed by leavetaking even though they had experienced daily leavetakings since early infancy (16 percent of toddlers cried as opposed to 8 percent of infants, and 20 percent of toddlers clung to their parents as opposed to 8 percent of infants). Their distress behavior decreased over the semester. The infants, however, showed increasing amounts of clinging and hovering across the two semesters. These data suggest that leavetaking distress may be related more to age than to experience with leavetakings. Greater distress was also observed among the female infants and toddlers. This may partially relate to the parents' behaviors. Most of the girls were brought by their mothers, while several of the boys were brought by their fathers. Children dropped off by their mothers cried and tried to get their attention more, and mothers hovered and lingered more, upsetting the children.

Mothers' leavetakings may be more stressful because

they worry more about them. In one study, 40 percent of the mothers and none of the fathers worried about their infants' responses to departures, and 75 percent of the mothers but only 35 percent of the fathers expected their infants to cry (Weinraub and Lewis 1977). Parents behave consistent with their worries and expectations, and their behavior may reinforce their children's. Hovering around and attempting to distract the child seems to encourage the child's crying. Infants and toddlers who hovered around their parents, tried to get their attention, protested verbally, clung, and cried had parents who hovered around them, tried to distract them, and sneaked out of the classroom. The children who hovered and verbally protested during leavetaking often continued play when their parents arrived to pick them up. On the other hand, the children who were more likely to move toward classroom activities during leavetaking and not hover around their parents were more likely to greet their parents and encourage them to depart at the end of the day. Certain children may have more trouble leaving an attachment figure, whether the parent in the morning or the peers and teacher in the afternoon. Others may simply have trouble adapting to change.

Despite the occasional distress shown by infants and toddlers during leavetaking, any parent who has peeked through the door or observed through a one-way window knows that crying and protest cease almost immediately after the parent's departure. Infants and toddlers new to daycare require a period of adjustment as they become acquainted with their peers and teachers. However, most of this time they are not upset. One study investigated behavior in children between the ages of two and three entering a nursery school for the first time (Fox and Field 1989). Data were collected by parental reports and investigator's observations of the children. The parents reported increased sleep disturbances one week before school started. The sleep problems disappeared after the first week of school and no further problems in this or any other area were reported by the parents. The increase in sleep problems may relate to anxiety on the part of the children about starting school. The anxiety had apparently decreased when the sleep disturbances disappeared. There is a similar pattern of behavior when preschoolers were transferred to new schools (Field 1984). Those children also showed sleep disturbances before their transfer which rapidly disappeared following the transfer.

A second pattern that appeared in this study was the change in both solitary and interactive behavior over the first six weeks of school. During the first two weeks the children were solitary much of the time (aimlessly wandering, following others around, playing alone, and remaining close to the teacher) and involved very little in interactive play. This pattern reversed itself by the end of the six week observation period. Some interesting individual differences also appeared. Children with high activity levels and greater sleep disturbances prior to school engaged in less interactive play and more solitary play during the first two weeks of school. However, these children showed a greater increase in interactive play over the first six weeks of school. The pattern of increasing interactive play and decreasing solitary behavior may be seen as an active coping response for children in this novel environment. Because learning to play with peers is one of the major milestones for nursery school children, this response was considered a positive development.

PEER ATTACHMENT

We know infants and toddlers are attached to their peers because they become distressed when they are separated, very much as they do during separations from parents. The transitions from one nursery school class to another provide a natural context for studying early peer separations. A group of infants and a group of toddlers, each of which had been together for several months, were observed for one month preceding and one month following their graduation to the next class (Field 1986; Field et al. 1986). These groups of infants and toddlers had been together as classmates in an all-day nursery program since they were one to three months old. Infants and toddlers were routinely graduated to the toddler class at fifteen months, and toddlers moved into preschool at twenty-four months. During the pre-separation period (a week before the transfer), as compared to observations made four weeks before it, there was more fussing, physical contact (both affection and aggression), wandering, and fantasy play. In addition, activity level was higher during this period, as was absenteeism (Figure 5.1). These measures remained elevated during the post-separation period (one week after the transfer) but had decreased by the time of follow-up (one month later). The children had more sleep problems and cried more often during the separation period. Their parents also reported a greater number of disturbances in sleeping, toilet behavior, and health during the pre- and post-separation periods (Figures 5.2 and 5.3).

Infants and toddlers who graduated with close friends were less stressed than those who did not, suggesting that transferring with close friends served as a buffer for

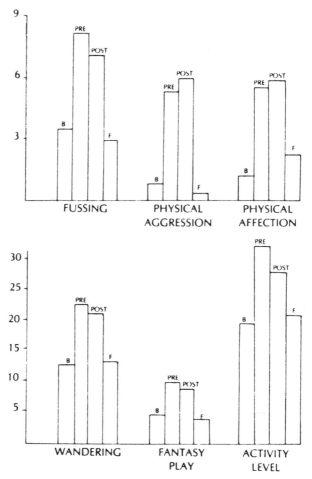

Figure 5.1. Changes in the proportion of time spent in various behaviors and in activity level of infants and toddlers associated with separation from peers. B, baseline; PRE, preseparation; POST, postseparation; F, follow-up.

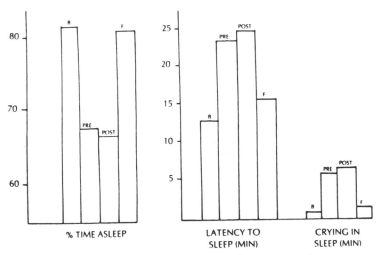

Figure 5.2. Changes in percentage of nap time spent asleep, latency to sleep, and crying in sleep in infants and toddlers associated with separation from peers. B, baseline; PRE, preseparation; POST, postseparation; F, follow-up.

separation distress. The infants and toddlers who graduated with close friends showed less fussing, physical aggression, and aimless wandering. They also cried less before naptime and spent a greater percentage of their naptime sleeping. Fewer sleep problems were also noted by the parents of infants and toddlers who transferred with their close friends.

It is interesting that the toddlers showed more distress prior to separation while the infants showed more distress following the separation. This suggests that toddlers have the necessary cognitive development to anticipate the stress associated with separation. The toddlers may have been responding to teachers' and parents' reminders about the upcoming graduation, and they may have remembered those children who had

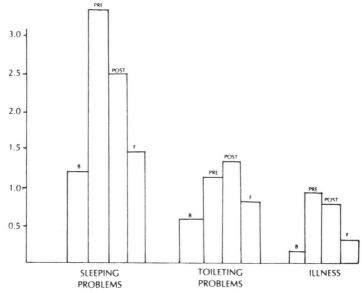

Figure 5.3. Number of problems with sleeping, toileting, and illness in infants and toddlers associated with separation from peers. B, baseline; PRE, preseparation; POST, postseparation; F, follow-up.

graduated the previous month and never returned to the classroom. Also, they may have remembered their own graduation from the infant nursery nine months earlier. Finally, they may have experienced anticipatory fear of their new, less familiar teachers and the bigger and more skillful classmates they had seen on their common playground. Nonetheless, the distress observed in these children was very short-lived; the follow-up observation yielded data very similar to those from the pre-separation observation.

Early experience with peers and daycare or nursery school settings does not seem to interfere with the infants' attachment to their parents. Instead, infants appear to develop multiple attachments to parents and peers. The more early contact they have with peers, for example in infant daycare, the more socially interactive they become.

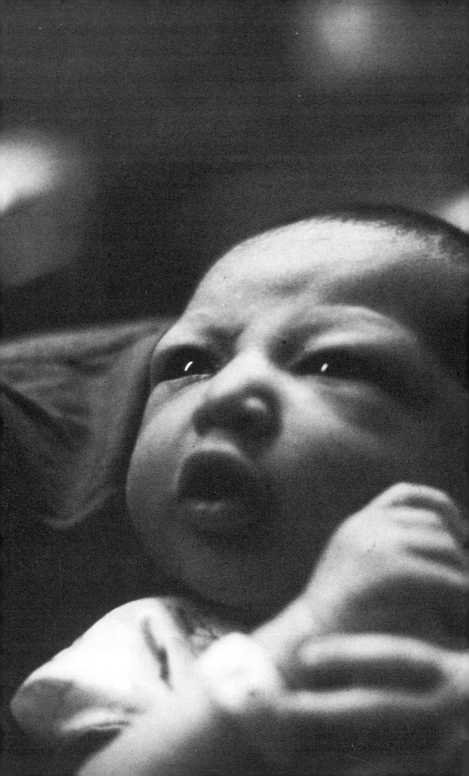

6/ Infants at Risk

Infants are considered at risk if they experience an undesirable prenatal or birth condition or if they are exposed to an early postnatal environment that might
contribute to early interaction problems and developmental delays. Undesirable prenatal conditions include
maternal disease and use of drugs, alcohol, or tobacco.
Problems at birth that might lead to difficulties include
premature or postmature delivery, low birthweight, and
the presence of congenital anomalies such as Down syndrome, craniofacial defects, deafness, blindness, and
autism. Postnatal environments that include a mother
who is a low-income teenager, neglectful or abusive, or
postpartum depressed might lead to developmental
problems. After a brief review of prenatal risk factors,
this discussion will focus on the conditions of prematurity and postpartum depression.

PRENATAL RISK FACTORS

DISEASES

Maternal diseases that can negatively affect prenatal
development include German measles, sexually transmitted diseases such as syphilis, gonorrhea, and herpes

simplex, and AIDS. Other conditions such as high blood pressure, diabetes, and blood incompatibilities may also have negative effects on the fetus. The negative effects of German measles typically occur during early pregnancy and can result in blindness and deafness. Sexually transmitted diseases usually affect the more mature fetus. Gonorrhea and herpes simplex are thought to affect the infant during the birth process, resulting in damage to the eyes and central nervous system. Silver nitrate drops in the eyes of newborns can prevent blindness from gonorrhea and Caesarean delivery prevents the infant from contracting herpes during delivery.

A substantial number of women of childbearing age may now be infected with the HIV virus, through sexual transmission or other modes of infection. Of pediatric AIDS cases, 77 percent were acquired perinatally; between 70 and 80 percent of these cases are related to intravenous drug abuse in the child's mother or her sexual partner (Ammann 1987; Curran et al. 1988). The time at which HIV infection of the fetus or the infant by the mother occurs is not yet known. Opportunities for transmission occur in utero, during labor or delivery, and postnatally through nursing or other forms of contact. Infection appears most likely to occur in utero, although it may also occur during delivery through exposure to maternal blood. Infants can also be infected by blood transfusion during the postpartum period. Infants exposed perinatally to HIV typically show symptoms of AIDS at about four to six months (Minkoff et al. 1987). Disease and death are very high in children with HIV infection. The mortality rate is approximately 80 percent and prolonged and repeated hospitalizations are common (Scott et al. 1985). In addition, as many as 96 percent of infected children followed to age four have central nervous system dysfunction (Belman et al.

1988). Of these, 43 percent had mild developmental delays and as many as 50 percent were within the moderate to severe range. This disease is clearly one of the greatest risks to infants.

DRUGS

The ingestion of drugs, both therapeutic and recreational, during pregnancy has received considerable attention. The potential dangers of taking prescription drugs during pregnancy were highlighted in the 1960s by the Thalidomide disaster, in which women who had taken a mild sedative while pregnant gave birth to children with severe abnormalities of the limbs. Since then it has become known that many kinds of medication, from tranquilizers and anticonvulsants to high doses of aspirin, may cause harm to the developing fetus. Nonetheless, during pregnancy the American woman on average consumes six prescription and four over-the-counter drugs (Arena 1979). Pregnant women and their physicians must carefully weigh the benefits of medication against possible risks to the fetus.

Recreational drugs such as LSD, heroin, methadone, cocaine, and crack also have deleterious effects on the fetus and newborn. Infants born to mothers who are heroin or morphine addicts are often premature and underweight, and typically experience withdrawal symptoms such as irritability, vomiting, trembling, shrill crying, rapid breathing, and hyperactivity (Householder et al. 1982). Paradoxically, methadone, the very drug that is used to treat heroin addiction, produces more severe withdrawal symptoms in infants than heroin does. Little is known about the effects of the more recently widespread drug cocaine and its crack form, although it appears to result in less severe withdrawal symptoms in newborns than narcotics produce (Finnegan 1988). Follow-up studies at four months of age have found motor development delays in infants whose mothers consumed cocaine or crack during pregnancy (Burns and Burns 1988).

It is difficult to determine how much of the risk to infants of drug-abusing mothers is related to prenatal exposure to the drug and how much to maternal deprivation. Women who abuse drugs tend to be depressed and lack good models for parenting. These factors combine with the neurological and behavioral deficits of drug-exposed newborns to put them at high risk for continuing developmental problems. The social environment of the drug-abused infant has been highly implicated in developmental delays. One of the very few follow-up studies on children of drug-addicted mothers (addicted in this case to heroin) compared the effects of the drug's being taken before and after the birth of the infant (Wilson et al. 1979). No differences were found between the effects of exposure to drugs in utero and the effects of exposure after birth to the social environment of the drug-using caretakers, suggesting the potent effects of the drug-abusing environment.

One element of this environment is maternal depression. Several studies have documented depression in opiate-abusing mothers, using the Beck Depression Inventory or its short form (Burns et al. 1985; Regan et al. 1980). In samples that ranged from 47 to 149 women, these studies together found on average that 20 percent were mildly depressed, 38 percent moderately depressed, and 17 percent severely depressed—that is, more than 50 percent of these women were moderately to severely depressed. These results are perhaps not surprising, considering these mothers' social problems, which may include poverty, legal problems, homelessness, lack of social supports, loss of children to foster care, and frequently abusive relationships with drug-abusing or alcoholic men.

It is noteworthy that these depression scores were obtained during pregnancy and prior to the placement of these women's children in foster care, given the increasing incidence of foster care placement (approximately 40 percent of children of drug-abusing mothers) and given that higher depression scores are typically noted among women whose children are placed in foster homes than among those who retain custody of them (Burns and Burns 1988). It is difficult to determine whether the foster placement is an antecedent or a consequence of the depression. Non-drug-abusing women during acute episodes of depression have been observed to be less involved with their children, and in general to have impaired communication, increased friction, lack of affection, and greater guilt and resentment. These women were also overprotective, irritable, preoccupied, withdrawn, emotionally distant, and rejecting. In cases of maternal drug abuse the potential for interactional difficulties is greater than with many other high-risk mothers because the drug abuse affects both the mother and the infant, and both members of the dyad begin their relationship in a vulnerable state.

ALCOHOL AND TOBACCO

Alcohol and tobacco are considered by most women as less harmful to the fetus than narcotic drugs. However, these drugs also have undesirable prenatal effects (Stechler and Halton 1982). Despite considerable public attention to the effects of these drugs, it is estimated that in the United States, during pregnancy, over 80 percent of women drink alcohol and 57 percent smoke cigarettes. Women who smoke or drink tend to have higher rates of spontaneous abortion, prematurity, and low birthweight babies. In addition, sudden infant death syndrome is more common in the offspring of mothers who smoke or drink than in those of women who do not. Because smoking and drinking often go together, it is difficult to determine their independent effects; nonetheless, chronic smoking alone almost doubles the incidence of prematurity, and full-term babies of smokers have lower birthweights.

Approximately one-third of infants of alcoholic mothers have what is called "fetal alcohol syndrome." This syndrome is characterized by facial, heart, and limb defects as well as below-average growth and, frequently, mental retardation. In addition, these infants exhibit abnormal behaviors such as excessive irritability, hyperactivity, distractibility, and tremulousness, and stereotyped motor behaviors such as head banging and body rocking (Pierog et al. 1977). Still other problems include feeding disturbances and mild-to-severe speech and language difficulties. The syndrome is thought to result from the effects of alcohol on the brain during prenatal development.

If drinking and smoking cease during the later months of pregnancy, the babies appear to be longer, weigh more, and have larger head circumference than those whose mothers continue the habits. The effects of these drugs do not appear to be limited to the newborn period. Thirteen-month-old infants of mothers who drank moderately during pregnancy score lower on tests of motor and language development. At four and seven years of age those children whose mothers had drunk heavily during pregnancy had more difficulty sitting still and paying attention and had lower IQ scores (Streissguth et al. 1984, 1986, 1989).

Malnutrition is thought to be one of the underlying mechanisms responsible for the growth deficiencies of infants whose mothers used alcohol or tobacco. Mothers who smoke and drink are less likely to have good prenatal nutrition, which deprives the fetus. Insufficient prenatal vitamins, protein, and iron are related to increased rates of abortion, prematurity, stillbirth, infant mortality, and physical and neurological defects. Another possible effect of both tobacco and alcohol is the restriction of oxygen to the fetus. The same condition is seen in babies born at high altitudes or born prematurely. The symptoms of these babies are not unlike those of the offspring of mothers who drink and smoke.

MATERNAL ANXIETY

Literally dozens of studies have linked maternal anxiety during pregnancy to less than optimal outcomes (Stechler and Halton 1982). Maternal anxiety is related to greater fetal activity; at birth, infants are hyperactive and more irritable, cry more, and have more feeding and sleeping problems (Stanley et al. 1979). Stresses during pregnancy that have been related to maternal anxiety include marital discord, the death of a husband, and unwanted pregnancy. Intense pregnancy anxiety has been related to fear that the child will be born with Down syndrome or a cleft lip and palate. Because anxiety is often accompanied by smoking and drinking, these activities may contribute to the effects related to anxiety. Maternal anxiety may also continue in the postpartum period and contribute to the hyperactivity and irritability of the newborn.

A recent study attempted to alleviate anxiety about pregnancy by giving video and verbal feedback during ultrasound assessments to assure the mother of the well-being of her fetus (Field et al. 1985). This intervention was effective in altering the course of fetal and infant development. Compared to infants whose mothers did not receive such feedback, the infants in the study were less active in utero and had higher birthweights. As newborns they were less irritable and their performance on neonatal behavior assessments was superior. Thus, it would appear that simply reassuring the mother of fetal well-being has positive effects on the fetus and newborn.

PREMATURITY

Prematurity or preterm delivery, defined as delivery prior to thirty-seven weeks' gestation, happens to approximately 250,000 infants per year in the United States. Approximately half of all women who deliver prematurely go into premature labor for unknown reasons; the remaining women have diagnosed conditions such as toxemia, incompetent cervix, or placenta previa. A woman who has had a premature baby has a 25–50 percent chance of premature delivery in each subsequent pregnancy. Although the survival rates among these infants are an excellent 90–98 percent, conditions that occur during the neonatal period such as respiratory distress syndrome and infection can pose a threat. In addition, premature infants experience developmental delays over the first few years of life, and some have later learning disabilities.

MEDICAL PROBLEMS

The primary medical problem of prematurity is the immaturity of the infant's organs. Birth stresses are not easily tolerated by the preterm infant. Smaller newborns tend to be delivered rapidly and are subjected to abrupt changes in pressure in the birth canal. Bruising or internal bleeding often occurs. The stresses of labor may cause the premature infant to be born deprived of oxygen and unable to begin breathing on its own. Outside the womb, the preemie is susceptible to hypothermia (chilling) and infection. The preterm infant may also develop hypoglycemia (low glucose) and thus tire easily.

The most common problem facing a newborn preterm infant is immaturity of the lungs, specifically the inability to produce enough surfactant to keep the lungs expanded as it breathes, a condition known as respiratory distress syndrome, or RDS. The baby with RDS has difficulty switching from the fetal pattern of respiration and circulation to the postnatal pattern. Nonoxygenated blood circulates through the body and the baby's tissues become oxygen deprived. The production of surfactant can be disrupted by stresses during birth, including oxygen deprivation, blood loss, or low blood pressure, hypothermia, or hypoglycemia. Because these stresses increase the infant's vulnerability to RDS and other serious conditions, the infant and mother are typically monitored during labor and delivery, either with an external monitor on the mother's abdomen or by an internal monitor placed on the baby's scalp. These devices monitor the baby's heart rate, which indicates its stress level. If the infant becomes stressed it is typically delivered by Caesarean section.

A preemie who is receiving oxygen therapy has frequent blood tests to determine the amount of oxygen in the bloodstream. In order to withdraw the blood easily, a catheter is threaded through the umbilical artery into the aorta, the main artery supplying the body with oxygenated blood. Fluids, nutrients, blood, and medications can also be given through the umbilical catheter.

A preemie who continues to breathe well for the first two or three days after delivery is less likely to develop respiratory distress syndrome. However, it is still vulnerable to other problems such as jaundice, feeding difficulties, infection, unstable body temperature, and irregular breathing or heart rate. For these reasons the preemie is kept in intensive care, separate from the mother. Although most conditions of prematurity can be effectively treated, the extensive paraphernalia surrounding the infant limits parent-infant contact. Hoods for providing oxygen, intubation for respiration, intravenous feeding apparatus, and nasogastric tubes for feeding, as well as the many devices for monitoring the infant's vital signs, make the preemie look fragile and "wired-up." Although most neonatology units suggest that only parental illness should prevent contact with the infant, the infant looks too fragile to handle. In addition, parents are troubled by its lack of resemblance to a "Gerber baby" and reluctant to become attached given the possibility that the infant may not survive.

DEVELOPMENTAL PROBLEMS

One of the biggest problems the premature infant presents to its parents is its immature development. The preemie may have difficulty looking, listening, and remembering to breathe at the same time. Its neurological circuits are easily overloaded by the constant stimulation of lights, sounds, and sensations. When tired or overly excited it may have spells of forgetting to breathe (apnea) and low heart rate (bradycardia). Because of an immature nervous system and poor muscle tone, the preemie's movements are weak and poorly controlled. The arms and legs move about in a disorganized fashion, with frequent jerks and startles. It dozes restlessly in what is called "active" sleep, characterized by uneven breathing, irregular heart rate, and rapid eye movement under closed lids. The infant's behavior is similar to that of a dreaming adult; it may gasp, cry out, smile, or grimace in rapid succession. Reflex smiling is also common. Much of the preemie's behavior is inconsistent, puzzling, and distressing to adults. The infant may not give clear signals when it wants to eat or sleep, when it has had too much stimulation or not enough; it may be excessively fussy or spend most of the time asleep. Parents, in turn, may avoid or overstimulate the baby, further worsening its behavior and their own frustration.

Despite the medical complications that preterm infants experience—especially serious for those who weigh less than 1500 grams or 3-½ pounds at birth—most of these infants do not experience long-term developmental effects. When the developmental progress of preterm infants is periodically evaluated during infancy and childhood, the age of the preterm infant is adjusted for prematurity, and test scores are compared to normal values for a child of that age. For example, an infant born three months early would be compared at fifteen months to a one-year-old infant born at full term. Later in childhood the weeks or months of prematurity become less significant.

At the end of the first year, investigators have noted significant problems in about 10 percent of prematurely born infants. Fewer than 5 percent are seriously disabled by blindness, profound retardation, or severe cerebral palsy. The other 5 percent have lesser degrees of retardation, mild to moderate cerebral palsy, or visual and hearing impairments.

By age six an additional 28 percent of the children show evidence of milder problems that require special education. These include learning disabilities, behavior disorders, problems with physical coordination, and lower than normal IQ. Some of these children exhibit a combination of characteristics referred to as minimal brain dysfunction or hyperactivity. Hyperactive children tend to behave impulsively, have a low tolerance for frustration, and have poor emotional control. They may have shorter attention spans and be easily distractable. They may be hypersensitive to lights, sounds, and other sensory stimulation. Their learning disabilities involve problems with hand-eye coordination and visual perception. Because of these problems drawing, reading, and writing present special challenges. Some children also have problems with speech and self-expression. These learning disabilities exist in children of all IQ levels.

Despite these problems most prematurely born infants although they have significantly lower scores on infant tests such as the Bayley scales, by four and five years have IQ scores well within the normal range (Hunt 1981; Siegel 1983; Field et al. 1983). In addition, the majority of prematurely born infants—at least 60 percent—do not have even mild problems.

SUPPLEMENTAL STIMULATION

Concern about giving preterm infants the best start has led to the introduction of several forms of supplemental stimulation in the intensive care nursery. Premature infants, who are deprived of their final weeks in utero, may also be deprived of appropriate stimulation after birth. The environment of the incubator features bright lights and continuous noise, and the newborns are handled infrequently and only briefly. Although the effects of this environment are virtually unknown at this point, some have suggested that the neonatal intensive care nursery may constitute a source of sensory deprivation. Others have suggested that preterm neonates may be overstimulated or at the very least may experience inappropriate patterns of stimulation (Gottfried and Gaiter 1985; Cornell and Gottfried 1976).

Stimulation experiences provided for preterm newborns are designed to mimic either the environment of the womb or that of the outside world. Some have viewed the preterm neonate as more like a fetus, while others consider that the preterm neonate differs from the fetus because the sensory systems undergo physiological changes at birth. Different forms of stimulation may be necessary for postnatal development regardless of gestational age.

Stimulation is usually begun as soon as possible after birth and continues until the infant is discharged from the hospital. In some studies auditory stimulation has been provided in the form of a heartbeat sound or a recording of the mother's voice. However, most studies have featured touching and movement stimulation, including various combinations of handling, rocking, or stroking, preferably involving the parents (Ransch 1981; Rice 1977; White and Labarba 1976; Levy-Schiff et al. 1989). Most of these studies have cited benefits for the infants from all types of intervention, ranging from weight gain to better performance on developmental assessments. Assessments of motor abilities, in particular, both at birth and on developmental tests throughout the first year, consistently suggest an advantage for the stimulated infants. Since the most frequently reported delays experienced by preterm infants are motor delays, it is noteworthy that the extra stimulation appears to facilitate motor development. Prolonged effects have been most clearly demonstrated by programs that have continued stimulation after discharge to the infant's home, in which mothers are taught stimulation exercises and invited to perform them daily. Although the effects reported for these programs may be partly the result of greater involvement of the parents with their infants, they are notably more persistent than those of programs terminating at hospital discharge.

Two simple and inexpensive stimulation programs are nonnutritive sucking during tube feedings and infant massage. Although sucking is a natural activity, opportunities to do so are not usually provided for infants who are fed by nasogastric tubes. Sucking on a pacifier during tube feedings may facilitate later bottle feeding. In one study pacifiers were given to very premature, low birthweight infants during all tube feedings (Field et al. 1982). Infants in the treatment group required fewer days of tube feedings. In addition, they averaged more weight gain per day, were hospitalized for fewer days, and had significantly lower hospital costs. They also experienced fewer medical problems and were easier to feed during later bottle feedings. Finally, their weight and head circumferences at one year were greater than those of infants who did not receive stimulation.

Another program involved massaging preterm neonates (Field et al. 1986). A group of infants was massaged for three fifteen-minute periods during three consecutive hours each day for ten days. Each stimulation session had three five-minute phases. During the first and third phases (tactile stimulation), the infant was placed on its stomach and stroked on the head and face, neck and shoulders, back, legs, and arms. The middle phase (kinesthetic stimulation) involved flexing of the infant's limbs while the infant was lying on its back. The stimulated infants averaged 47 percent greater weight gain per day, even though they did not differ from the control group in number of feedings or average formula intake (Figure 6.1). They were also awake and active a greater percentage of the time and showed more

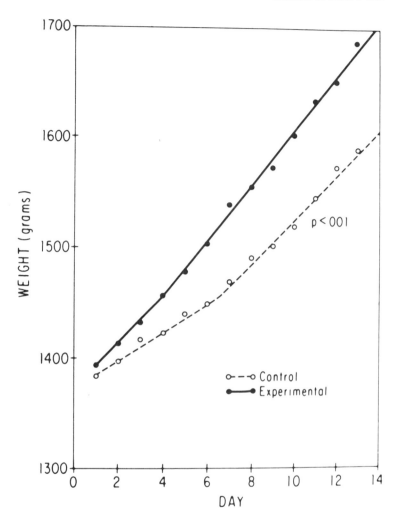

Figure 6.1. Mean daily weight gain of premature infants who received massage (experimental group) and those who did not (control).

mature behaviors on the Brazelton Neonatal Scale. In addition they were hospitalized six days less than the control infants, yielding an average hospital cost savings of $3,000 per infant. Finally, follow-up assessment at six to eight months indicated higher weight and better performance on the Bayley mental and motor scales.

Thus, it would appear that interventions of this kind seem to facilitate the growth and development of preterm infants. It should be noted that individual infants may require different amounts of stimulation. Programs that are effective for some infants are not necessarily effective for others. Finally, stimulation programs may be more effective if the parents, who will continue to be the primary source of stimulation for the infants, are involved in the intervention program.

MATERNAL DEPRESSION

Studying the effects of maternal depression on infant development is important because of its high incidence: 10–12 percent of mothers experience postpartum depression and 40–70 percent have postpartum blues, with the effects lasting beyond one year in approximately 4 percent, and a recurrence rate of 20–30 percent. Recent evidence suggests that women who are not clinically depressed but have high levels of depressive symptoms may exhibit more stable pathology than clinically depressed women. These women may place their infants at particularly high risk. Less favorable emotional development has been reported for children reared by depressed mothers as opposed to those raised by mothers who have other diagnoses or are normal (Sameroff and Seifer 1983). In addition, early interaction disturbances are related to later childhood problems (Bakeman and Brown 1980).

Face-to-face interactions of depressed mothers and their infants have been compared to the interactions of nondepressed mothers and their infants (Field 1984; Bettes 1988). The depressed mothers showed fewer positive facial expressions, more negative expressions, and fewer vocalizations, and looked at and touched their infants less. The depressed mothers' infants, in turn, showed fewer positive facial expressions, more negative facial expressions, fewer vocalizations, more gaze aversion, more protesting, and lower activity levels. The behavior of these infants suggests that by frequent exposure to their mothers' depressed behaviors the infants developed a depressed style of interacting. It is not known whether the depressed affect of these infants is a result of mirroring their mothers' behavior or a result of the minimal stimulation provided by the mothers. Very little is known about the genetic transmission of depression. It is possible that there is a genetic predisposition for depression, given that infants of depressed mothers are at an unusually high risk for developing depression.

One possibility is that these infants were depressed from birth. In another study mothers who had been depressed during pregnancy were filmed interacting with their infants when they were three months old (Field et al. 1985). As newborns the infants were given a Brazelton assessment and noted to have depressed activity levels and limited responses to social stimulation. This behavior continued at three months. The infants showed fewer contented expressions and were fussier during their interactions. Because the mothers' prenatal depression continued into the postpartum period, they were less active with their infants and showed fewer positive facial expressions, fewer imitative behaviors, and less game-playing with their infants. Again, it is not clear whether the infant's depression was merely a behavioral style that persisted from birth or one that developed from prolonged exposure to the mother's depression.

The infants of these mothers are depressed in mood and behavior even when their mothers do not behave in a depressed fashion. Although most clinicians think of depression behavior as withdrawn and inactive, some depressed mothers have a more intrusive interaction style (Cohn et al. 1986). Whether the mother is withdrawn or intrusive, the infants of depressed mothers seem to respond more to their mothers' negative behavior while the infants of nondepressed mothers are more responsive to their mothers' positive behavior, thus mirroring or mimicking their mothers' predominant mood states (Figures 6.2 and 6.3). This is very disturbing because the infants' depressed behavior is not limited to interactions with their depressed mothers. Another study observed three-month-old infants of depressed mothers interacting with nondepressed women as well as with their mothers (Field et al. 1988). The infants of depressed mothers received low interaction ratings with the nondepressed women that were very similar to ratings for their interactions with their mothers. This suggests that the infants' depressed style extends to their interactions with nondepressed adults. Whatever the origins of this behavior, its persistence regardless of interaction partners is disturbing.

Early infant interaction behavior is related to later peer interaction behavior and performance on developmental assessments. Infants of depressed mothers are at risk for developmental problems in a number of areas (Radke-Yarrow 1985; Gaensbauer et al. 1984; Zahn-

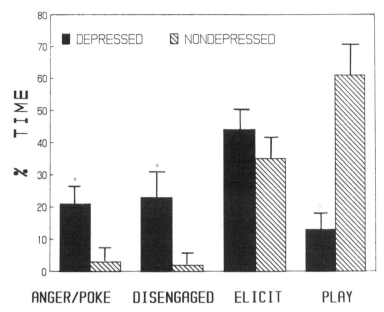

Figure 6.2. Percentage of time spent in various behaviors toward their infants by depressed and nondepressed mothers.

Waxler 1984; Sameroff et al. 1982). On the positive side, however, it seems that the infant can recover if the mother recovers from her postpartum depression. Some preliminary data suggest that mothers who remain depressed over the infants' first six months of life have infants who develop a depressed style of interacting. However, if the mothers were no longer depressed at six months, the infants were also no longer depressed. Although these data suggest the profound effect of maternal depression on infant behavior, they also highlight the adaptability and resilience of infants. If mood states are shared, it is not surprising that the infant's mood states may change as the mother's moods change.

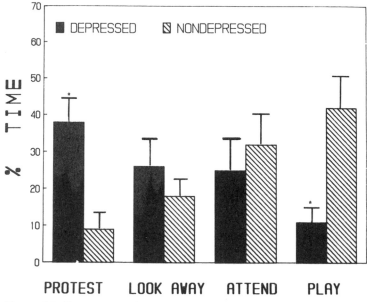

Figure 6.3. Percentage of time spent in various behaviors toward their mothers by infants of depressed and nondepressed mothers.

INTERACTION DISTURBANCES AND INTERACTION COACHING

The interactions of high-risk infants with their mothers and of high-risk mothers with their infants are characterized by lack of excitement and responsivity. Such early interaction disturbances are related to later school-age behavioral and emotional problems, including hyperactivity, limited attention span, and disturbed peer interactions, as well as to emotional disturbances diagnosed as depression (Widmayer et al.). A series of studies has demonstrated the disturbances that occur during early interactions when the mother is unable to read her infant's signals and provide optimal stimulation. Interactions with high-risk infants are particularly challenging. High-risk infants spend less time looking at their mothers and appear to enjoy their interactions less than normal infants. Their smiles and vocalizations are less frequent and they fuss and cry more frequently than normal infants. The greater incidence of negative affective displays among these infants together with their elevated heart rates suggests that their interactions may be stressful. Their elevated heart rate, gaze aversion, and negative affect may reflect elevated arousal due to an information overload and excessive stimulation.

In their natural attempts to elicit positive affect, mothers of high-risk infants often provide too much stimulation and fail to vary their stimulation as their infants become distressed. For example, preterm infants seem to be unable to control erratic body movements and vocalizations and show more frequent shifts in their alertness (McGehee and Eckerman 1983). They also fuss and cry more and are more difficult to soothe. There appears to be a vicious cycle: the parent becomes more active as the infant remains inactive and unresponsive. The parents' activity is counterproductive because it leads to less instead of more response from the infant. A similar pattern has been observed in the interactions of Down syndrome, cerebral palsied, blind, deaf, autistic, and failure-to-thrive infants (Jones 1977; Fraiberg 1974; Massie 1978; Greenberg 1971).

The most vague explanation of this behavior is that the frustration of receiving a minimal response from the infant leads to aggressivity on the part of the mother. Another notion is that the mothers are more active to compensate for the relative inactivity of their infants, perhaps to keep some semblance of an interaction going. A third relates to the mother's wanting her child to perform like the child's age-mates and attempting to encourage performance by more frequent modeling of behaviors. Still another interpretation is that the mothers view their infants as fragile and delayed and as a result tend to be overprotective, which in the extreme results in overcontrolling behavior.

The infants' responsivity can be improved when mothers modify their behaviors (Clark and Seifer 1983; Field 1983). "Interaction coaching" is a term used for attempts to modify these disturbed interactions. A number of manipulations seem helpful. The manipulations are designed to enhance behaviors that are seen in more harmonious interactions. For example, harmonious feedings typically feature the infant gazing at the mother while vigorously sucking, and the mother silently watching, reserving her words for the infant's breaks from sucking. The disturbed feeding is characterized by a fussy, distracted, slow-to-suck, gaze-averting infant and a constantly coaxing mother. Similarly, in harmonious face-to-face interactions with infants, parents slow down, exaggerate, and repeat their behaviors, respond by imitating or highlighting the infant's behaviors, take turns, and respect the infant's occasional breaks from the conversation. The infant typically looks attentive and sounds content. The disturbed face-to-face interaction features a gaze-averting, squirming, fussing infant and an overactive, intrusive, controlling, and frustrated parent.

Because adults' behaviors are more amenable to change than are infants', attempts to modify interactions have focused on them. Some of the most effective manipulations include asking the mother to count slowly to herself as she interacts, to imitate all of her infant's behaviors, to repeat her words slowly, or to be silent when her infant is sucking or looking away (Field

1977). These manipulations vary in their effectiveness, but each results in longer periods of eye contact, fewer distressed vocalizations, and less squirming on the part of the infant. Other effective interventions include teaching the mother age-appropriate games, coaching her through an interaction by an earpiece microphone, and replaying videotapes of interactions for her either with or without the investigators' running commentary (Field 1987). Although the interaction coaching techniques seem to alter the mother's behavior and the infant's responsivity, it is not clear how much this experience carries over into their day-to-day interactions. The state of the art is relatively undeveloped since we know very little about harmonious interactions, less about disturbed interactions, and even less about intervention techniques. Nonetheless, the efficacy of interaction coaching suggests that adults can be shown other ways to interact with their infants, and that infants can in turn show that they, too, can interact in other ways.

In summary, infants considered at risk because of birth conditions or exposure to undesirable parenting have considerable difficulties during early interactions. Very common examples are the preterm infant and the infant born to a depressed mother. Stimulation techniques such as infant massage and interaction coaching can significantly ameliorate these problems. The resilience of infants and the perseverance of parents both contribute to more optimal development.

Afterword

A book about something as exciting as infants should not end with the unhappy subjects of developmental delays, premature births, and depressed mothers. Rather, these last remarks should hold promise and suggest future directions.

Infants are amazingly resilient. This phenomenon has not been studied adequately because of our preoccupation with pathology. Stress and coping are becoming buzzwords in the field of infancy as they have been for the study of adults. Infants have extraordinary coping skills in the face of biological and environmental adversities. Volumes have been written recently on how infants cope with stress (Field et al. 1988, 1990; Garmezy and Rutter 1983; Karrakas 1990; Lewis and Worobey 1989). Infants use resourceful self-comforting behavior such as sucking, fussing, and sleeping to cope with stresses such as pain, fatigue, and frustration and even more sophisticated behavior such as gaze aversion to cope with unstimulating conversations.

How some infants come to be resilient and others vulnerable is not yet known. Certainly parents' attitudes and expectations play a role (Bendell, 1989). But the infant's personality and temperament must certainly play a role as well. Emily Werner followed a group of resilient infants at risk from perinatal stress and poverty for thirty years as a part of the Kauai longitudinal study (Werner 1988). Her research was designed to assess the impact of a variety of biological and psychosocial risk factors, stressful life events, and protective factors on development. Those factors which seemed to make children resilient included autonomy and a positive social orientation. In addition, all of the resilient children had an established bond with at least one caregiver.

One of the other individual temperament factors that may be found in resilient and invulnerable children is risk-taking behavior. Some infants are apprehensive in stressful situations, while more resilient infants appear either to be relatively immune to adverse stress effects or to interpret the situation as a challenge, as in risk-taking. High levels of curiosity and exploratory behavior in infants could be described as risk-taking behavior. The risk-taking infants seem to seek out novelty during the first few months and engage in extensive exploratory behavior by the end of the first year, behavior that can be interpreted as an active search for challenging situations. These children may learn more and develop more rapidly because of their curiosity and exploratory behavior. This risk-taking behavior would be particularly helpful for infants whose parents tend to be overprotective. Often these parents, who fear that their child will falter or fail, tend to be too active and directive when the child does not perform and tend to give up too easily and do for the child instead of challenging the child to use its own resources and take risks. In this situation a little stress and a little risk-taking behavior may be needed for the infant to become resilient and ultimately the agent of its own development.

Stress and coping, resilience, and risk-taking behavior in infancy are phenomena that need further study (Field 1989). Such study will undoubtedly provide further evidence of the amazing qualities and abilities of the infant.

References

1 / STUDYING INFANTS

Brazelton, T. B. 1973. *Neonatal behavioral assessment scale*. London: Spastics International Medical Publications.

Bruner, J. S. 1973. Pacifier-produced visual buffering in human infants. *Developmental Psychobiology*, 6: 45–51.

Darwin, C. 1877. A biographical sketch of an infant. *Mind*, 2: 285–294.

Darwin, C. 1965. *The Expression of the Emotions in Man and Animals*. Chicago: University of Chicago Press.

DeCasper, A. J., and W. P. Fifer. 1980. Of human bonding: Newborns prefer their mothers' voices. *Science*, 208: 1174–1176.

Dittrichova, J., and V. Lapackova. 1964. Development of the waking state in young infants. *Child Development*, 35: 365–370.

Fantz, R. L. 1966. Pattern discrimination and selective attention as determinants of perceptual development from birth. In A. H. Kidd and J. L. Riviore, eds., *Perceptual development in children*. New York: International University Press.

Field, T., N. Hallock, J. Dempsey, and H. H. Shuman. 1978. Mothers' assessments of term and preterm infants with Respiratory Distress Syndrome: Reliability and predictive validity. *Child Psychiatry and Human Development*, 9: 75–85.

Field, T., R. Woodson, D. Cohen, R. Garcia, and R. Greenberg. 1983. Discrimination and imitation of facial expressions by term and preterm neonates. *Infant Behavior and Development*, 6: 485–490.

Freud, S. 1949. *An outline of psychoanalysis*. New York: Norton.

Gardner, J., and H. Gardner. 1970. A note on selective imitation by a six-week-old infant. *Child Development*, 41: 1209–1213.

Goren, C. C., M. Sarty, and P. K. Wu. Visual following and pattern discrimination of facelike stimuli by newborn infants. *Pediatrics*, 56(4): 544–549.

Graham, F. K., and R. K. Clifton. 1966. Heart rate change as a component of the orienting response. *Psychological Bulletin*, 65: 305–320.

Hutt, S. J., C. Hutt, H. G. Lenard, H. V. Bernuth, and W. J. Muntjewerff. 1968. Auditory responsivity in the human neonate. *Nature*, 218: 888–890.

Kagan, J. 1967. The growth of the face schema: Theoretical significance and methodological issues. In J. Hellmuth, ed., *The exceptional infant*, vol. 1. Seattle: Brunner/Mazel.

Kagan, J., R. B. Kearsley, and P. R. Zelazo. 1978. *Infancy: Its place in human development*. Cambridge: Harvard University Press.

Lipsitt, L. P. 1988. Stress in infancy. In N. Garmezy and M. Rutter, eds., *Stress, coping and development in children*. Baltimore: Johns Hopkins University Press.

Maratos, O. 1973. "The origin and development of imitation in the first six months of life." Unpublished Ph.D. thesis, University of Geneva.

McCall, R. B. 1977. Challenges to a science of developmental psychology. *Child Development*, 48: 333–344.

Meltzoff, A. N., and M. K. Moore. 1977. Imitation of facial and manual gestures by human neonates. *Science*, 198: 75–78.

Nelson, M., R. Clifton, J. Dowd, and T. Field. 1978. Cardiac responding to auditory stimuli in newborn infants: Why pacifiers should not be used when heart rate is the major dependent variable. *Infant Behavior and Development*, 1: 277–290.

Parmelee, A. H., and E. Stern. 1972. Development of states in infants. In C. D. Clements, D. D. Purpura, and F. E. Mayer, eds., *Sleep and the maturing nervous system.* New York: Academic Press.

Piaget, J. 1952. *The origins of intelligence in children.* New York: International Universities Press.

Pomerleau-Malcuit, A., and R. K. Clifton. 1973. Neonatal heart rate response to tactile, auditory and vestibular stimulation in different states. *Child Development,* 44: 485–496.

Stern, D. N. 1985. *The Interpersonal World of the Infant.* New York: Basic Books.

Watson, J. B. 1928. *Psychological care of infant and child.* New York: Norton.

2 / BEFORE AND AFTER BIRTH

Adams, R. J., D. Mauer, and M. Davis. 1986. Newborns' discrimination of chromatic from achromatic stimuli. *Journal of Experimental Child Psychology,* 41: 267–281.

Akiyama, Y., F. Schulte, M. Schultz, and A. Parmelee. 1969. Acoustically evoked responses in premature and fullterm newborn infants. *Electroencephalography and Clinical Neurophysiology,* 26: 371–380.

Antell, S., and D. Keating. 1983. Perception of numerical invariance in neonates. *Child Development,* 54: 695–702.

Antell, S. E. G., and A. J. Caron. 1985. Neonatal perception of spatial relationships. *Infant Behavior and Development,* 8: 15–23.

Apgar, V. A., and L. S. James. 1962. Further observations on the newborn scoring system. *American Journal of Diseases of Children,* 104: 419–428.

Ashton, R. 1973. The influence of state and prandial condition upon the reactivity of the newborn to auditory stimulation. *Journal of Experimental Child Psychology,* 15: 315–327.

Balogh, R. D., and R. M. Porter. 1986. Olfactory preferences resulting from mere exposure in human neonates. *Infant Behavior and Development,* 9: 395–401.

Birnholz, J. C. 1981. Fetal eye movement patterns. *Science*, 213: 679–681.

Birnholz, J. C., and E. E. Farrell. 1984. Ultrasound images of human fetal development. *American Scientist*, 72: 608–613.

Bower, T. G. R. 1974. *Development in infancy*. San Francisco: W. H. Freeman.

Brazelton, T. B. 1973. Neonatal behavioral assessment scale. *Clinics in Developmental Medicine*, no. 50. Philadelphia: Lippincott.

Bushnell, I. W. R. 1987. "Neonatal recognition of the mother's face." Paper presented at the annual conference of the Developmental Psychology Section of the British Psychological Society, York.

Cernack, J. M., and R. H. Porter. 1985. Recognition of maternal axillary odors by infants. *Child Development*, 56: 1593–1598.

Condon, W., and L. Sander. 1974. Neonate movement is synchronized with adult speech: Interactional participation and language acquisition. *Science*, 183: 99–101.

Crook, C. K. 1978. Taste perception in the newborn infant. *Infant Behavior and Development*, 1: 52–69.

DeCasper, A. J., and W. P. Fifer. 1980. Of human bonding: Newborns prefer their mothers' voices. *Science*, 208: 1174–1176.

DeCasper, A. J., and A. D. Sigafoos. 1983. The intrauterine heartbeat: A potent reinforcer for newborns. *Infant Behavior and Development*, 6: 19–26.

DeCasper, A. J., and P. Prescott. 1984. Human newborns' perception of male voices: Preference, discrimination and reinforcing value. *Developmental Psychobiology*, 17: 481–491.

DeCasper, A. J., and M. J. Spence. 1986. Prenatal maternal speech influences newborns' perception of speech sounds. *Infant Behavior and Development*, 9: 133–150.

Dowd, J. M., and E. Z. Tronick. 1986. Temporal coordination of arm movements in early infancy: Do infants move in synchrony with adult speech? *Child Development*, 57: 762–776.

Dreyfus-Brisac, C. 1979. Neonatal electroencephalography. Pp. 397–472 in E. Scarpelli & E. Cosmi, eds., *Reviews in Perinatal Medicine*. New York: Raven Press.

Dunkeld, J., and T. G. R. Bower. 1976. "Infant response to impending optical collision." Unpublished manuscript, University of Edinburgh.

Dziurawiec, S., and H. D. Ellis. 1986. "Neonates' attention to face-like stimuli: Goren, Sarty and Wu (1975) revisited." Paper presented at the annual conference of the Developmental Psychology Section of the British Psychological Society, Exeter.

Ellingson, R. 1970. Variability of visually evoked responses in the human newborn. *Electroencephalography and Clinical Neurophysiology*, 29: 10–19.

Ellis, R. R., and R. J. Ellingson. 1973. Response to electrical stimulation to the median nerve in the human newborn. *Developmental Psychobiology*, 6: 235–244.

Engen, T., and L. P. Lipsitt. 1965. Decrement and recovery of responses to olfactory stimuli in the human neonate. *Journal of Comparative Physiological Psychology*, 56: 73–77.

Field, T., J. Dempsey, N. Hallock, and H. H. Shuman. 1978. Mothers' assessments of the behavior of their infants. *Infant Behavior and Development*, 1: 156–167.

Field, T., J. Dempsey, J. Hatch, G. Ting, and R. Clifton. 1979. Cardiac and behavioral responses to repeated tactile and auditory stimulation by preterm and term neonates. *Developmental Psychology*, 15: 406–416.

Field, T., and S. Widmayer. 1981. Developmental follow-up of infants delivered by Caesarean section and general anesthesia. *Infant Behavior and Development*, 3: 253–264.

Field, T., R. Woodson, R. Greenberg, and D. Cohen. 1982. Discrimination and imitation of facial expressions by neonates. *Science*, 218: 179–181.

Field, T., D. Cohen, R. Garcia, and R. Greenberg. 1984. Mother-stranger face discrimination by the newborn. *Infant Behavior and Development*, 7: 19–27.

Field, T., R. Greenberg, R. Woodson, D. Cohen, and R. Garcia. 1984. Facial expressions during Brazelton neonatal assessments. *Infant Mental Health Journal*, 5: 61–71.

Fischer, K. W., and A. Lazerson. 1984. A summary of prenatal development. In Fischer and Lazerson, *Human development*. New York: W. H. Freeman.

Ganchrow, J. R., J. E. Steiner, and M. Daher. 1983. Neonatal facial expressions in response to different qualities and intensities of gustatory stimuli. *Infant Behavior and Development*, 6: 473–484.

Gelman, S. R., S. Wood, W. N. Spellacy, and R. M. Abrams. 1982. Fetal movements in response to sound stimulation. *American Journal of Obstetrics and Gynecology*, 143(4): 484–485.

Gewirtz, J. L., A. R. Hollenbeck, and S. L. Sebris. 1979. "Mother-infant contact following vaginal delivery." Paper presented at the biennial meeting of the Society for Research in Child Development, San Francisco, California.

Gewirtz, J. L., and A. R. Hollenbeck. 1989. "Parent orientation and behavior to their neonates in the first month resulting from differential body contact/touch during the first postpartum hour." Paper presented at the Johnson & Johnson Pediatric Round Table, Miami, Florida.

Glass, P., G. Avery, K. Subramanian, et al. 1985. Effect of bright light in the hospital nursery on the incidence of retinopathy of prematurity. *New England Journal of Medicine*, 313: 401–404.

Goldberg, S. 1983. Parent-infant bonding: Another look. *Child Development*, 54: 1355–1382.

Goren, G. C., M. Sarty, and P. Y. K. Wu. 1975. Visual following and pattern discrimination of face-like stimuli by newborn infants. *Pediatrics*, 56: 544–549.

Hainline, L., E. Lemerise, I. Abramov, and J. Turkel. 1984. Orientational asymmetries in small-field optokinetic nystagmus in human infants. *Behavioral Brain Research*, 13: 217–230.

Humphrey, T. 1969. Postnatal repetition of human prenatal activity sequences with some suggestions of their neuroanatomical basis. Pp. 43–84 in K. J. Robinson, ed., *Brain and early behavior*. New York: Academic Press.

Humphrey, T. 1972. Central representation of the oral and facial areas of human fetuses. In J. F. Bosma, ed., *Third symposium on oral sensation and perception: The mouth of the infant*. Springfield, Ill.: Chas. C. Thomas.

Jacklin, C. N., M. E. Snow, and E. E. Maccoby. 1981. Tactile sensitivity and muscle strength in newborn boys and girls. *Infant Behavior and Development*, 4: 261–268.

Jones-Molfese, V. J. 1977. Responses of neonates to colored stimuli. *Child Development*, 48: 1092–1095.

Kaitz, M., A. Good, A. M. Rokem, and A. I. Eidelman. 1988. Mothers' and fathers' recognition of their newborns' photographs during the postpartum period. *Journal of Development and Behavioral Pediatrics*, 9: 223–226.

Kaitz, M., O. Meschulach-Sarfaty, and J. Auerbach. 1988. A reexamination of newborn's ability to imitate facial expressions. *Developmental Psychology*, 24: 3–7.

Kisilevsky, B. S., and D. W. Muir. 1987. "Fetal response to sound and vibration." Poster presented at the Society for Research in Child Development Conference, Baltimore, Maryland.

Klaus, M. H., and J. H. Kennell. 1982. *Parent-infant bonding*. 2nd ed. St. Louis: Morsby.

Kochanevich-Wallace, P. M., K. McCluskey-Fawcett, N. E. Meck, and C. J. Simons. 1988. Method of delivery and parent-newborn interaction. *Journal of Pediatric Psychology*, 13: 213–221.

Lamb, M. E. 1982. Early contact and maternal-infant bonding: One decade later. *Pediatrics*, 70: 763–768.

Lester, B. M., H. Als, and T. B. Brazelton. 1982. Regional obstetric anesthesia and newborn behavior: A reanalysis toward synergistic effects. *Child Development*, 53: 687–692.

Madison, L. S., J. K. Madison, and S. A. Adubato. 1986. Infant behavior and development in relation to fetal movement and habituation. *Child Development*, 57: 1475–1482.

Martin, G. B., and R. D. Clark. 1982. Distress crying in neonates: Species and peer specificity. *Developmental Psychology*, 18: 3–9.

Mcfarlane, A. 1975. Olfaction in the development of social preferences in the human neonate. Pp. 103–113 in *Parent-infant interaction: CIBA symposium*, vol. 33. Amsterdam: CIBA Foundation.

Meltzoff, A. N., and M. K. Moore. 1977. Imitation of facial and manual gestures by human neonates. *Science*, 198: 75–78.

Meltzoff, A. N., and R. W. Borton. 1979. Intermodal matching by human neonates. *Nature*, 282: 403–404.

Murray, A. D., R. M. Dolby, R. L. Nation, and D. B. Thomas. 1981. Effects of epidural anesthesia on newborns and their mothers. *Child Development*, 52: 71–82.

Prechtl, H., and M. O'Brien. 1982. Behavioural states of the full-term newborn: The emergence of a concept. Pp. 52–73 in P. Stratton, ed., *Psychobiology of the newborn*. New York: Wiley.

Reissland, N. 1988. Neonatal imitation in the first hour of life: Observations in rural Nepal. *Developmental Psychology*, 24: 464–469.

Rieser, J., A. Yonas, and K. Wikner. 1976. Radial localization of odours by human newborns. *Child Development*, 47: 856–859.

Rochat, R. 1987. Mouthing and grasping in neonates: Evidence for the early detection of what hard and soft substances afford for action. *Infant Behavior and Development*, 10: 435–449.

Rodholm, M. 1981. Effects of father-infant postpartum contact in their interaction three months after birth. *Early Human Development*, 5: 79–86.

Rosenstein, D., and H. Oster. 1988. Differential facial responses to four basic tastes in newborns. *Child Development*, 59: 1555–1568.

Sadovsky, E., and W. Polishuk. 1977. Fetal movements in utero: Nature, assessment, prognostic value, timing of delivery. *Obstetrics and Gynecology*, 50: 49–55.

Sagi, A., and M. L. Hoffman. 1976. Empathetic distress in the newborn. *Developmental Psychology*, 12: 175–176.

Saigel, S., N. Nelson, K. Bennett, and M. Enkin. 1981. Observations on the behavioral state of newborn infants during the first hour of life: A comparison of infants delivered by the Leboyer and conventional methods. *American Journal of Obstetrics and Gynecology*, 139: 715–719.

Simner, M. L. 1971. Newborn's response to the cry of another infant. *Developmental Psychology*, 5: 136–150.

Slater, A., V. Morison, and D. Rose. 1983. Perception of shape by the new-born baby. *British Journal of Developmental Psychology*, 1: 135–142.

Slater, A., D. Rose, and V. Morison. 1984. New-born infants' perception of similarities and differences between two- and three-dimensional stimuli. *British Journal of Developmental Psychology*, 2: 287–294.

Sosa, R., J. Kennell, M. Klaus, S. Robertson, and J. Urrutia. 1980. The effect of a supportive companion on perinatal problems, length of labor and mother-infant interaction. *New England Journal of Medicine*, 303(11): 597–600.

Steiner, J. E. 1979. Human facial expressions in response to taste and smell stimulation. In H. W. Reese and L. P. Lipsitt, eds., *Advances in child development and behavior*, vol. 13. New York: Academic Press.

Wolff, P. 1965. The development of attention in young infants. *Annals of the New York Academy of Sciences*, 118: 815–830.

Yang, R., and T. C. Douthitt. 1974. Newborn responses to threshold tactile stimulation. *Child Development*, 45: 237–242.

3 / MOTOR DEVELOPMENT AND LEARNING

Baillargeon, R., and M. Graber. 1988. Evidence of location memory in 8-month-old infants in a nonsearch AB task. *Developmental Psychology*, 24: 502–511.

Bayley, N. 1969. *Bayley scales of infant development*. New York: The Psychological Corporation.

Blass, E. M., J. R. Granchiow, and J. E. Steiner. 1984. Classical conditioning in newborn humans 2–48 hours of age. *Infant Behavior and Development*, 7: 223–236.

Bower, T. G. R. 1982. *Development in infancy*. 2nd ed. San Francisco: Freeman.

Bower, T. G. R., J. Dunkeld, and J. G. Wishart. 1979. Infant perception of visually presented objects. *Science*, 208: 1137–1138.

Brackbill, Y. 1958. Extinction of the smiling response in the infants as a function of reinforcement. *Child Development*, 29: 115–124.

Brazelton, T. B. 1973. *Neonatal behavioral assessment scale*. Clinics in Developmental Medicine, no. 50. London: Heinemann.

Bruner, J. S. 1972. Nature and uses of immaturity. *American Psychologist*, 27: 687–708.

Cohen, L. B., J. S. Deloache, and R. A. Pearl. 1977. An examination of interference effects in infants' memory for faces. *Child Development*, 48: 88–96.

Darwin, C. 1877. A biographical sketch of an infant. *Mind*, 7: 285–294.

DeCasper, A. J., and W. P. Fifer. 1980. Of human bonding: Newborns prefer their mothers' voices. *Science*, 208: 1174–1176.

DeCasper, A. J., and M. J. Spence. 1986. Prenatal maternal speech influences newborns' perception of speech sounds. *Infant Behavior and Development*, 9: 133–150.

Fagan, J. F. 1971. Memory in the infant. *Journal of Experimental Child Psychology*, 9: 217–226.

Fagan, J. F. 1973. Infants' delayed recognition memory and forgetting. *Journal of Experimental Child Psychology*, 16: 424–450.

Fagan, J. F. 1977. Infant recognition memory: Studies in forgetting. *Child Development*, 48: 68–78.

Fagan, J. F. 1982. New evidence for the prediction of intelligence from infancy. *Infant Mental Health Journal*, 3: 219–228.

Fagan, J. F., and S. K. McGrath. 1981. Infant recognition memory and later intelligence. *Intelligence*, 5: 121–130.

Fagan, J. W., and P. S. Ohr. 1985. Temperament and crying in response to the violation of a learned expectancy in early infancy. *Infant Behavior and Development*, 8: 157–166.

Graham, F. K., and R. K. Clifton. 1966. Heart rate change as a component of the orienting response. *Psychological Bulletin*, 65: 305–320.

Hutt, C. 1970. Curiosity in young children. *Science Journal*, 6(2): 69–71.

Iannirubuerto, A. 1985. "Prenatal onset of motor patterns." Paper presented at the Conference on Motor Skill Acquisition in Children. NATO Advanced Study Institute, Maastricht, Netherlands.

Illingworth, R. S. 1973. *Basic developmental screening: 0–2 years.* Oxford: Blackwell Scientific.

Jersild, A. T. 1955. *Child psychology.* 4th ed. London: Staples Press.

Lipsitt, L. P., and H. Kaye. 1964. Conditioned sucking in the human newborn. *Psychonomic Science*, 1: 29–30.

McDonnell, P. M., V. E. S. Anderson, and W. C. Abraham. 1983. Asymmetry and orientation of arm movements in three-to-eight week old infants. *Infant Behavior and Development*, 6: 287–298.

Myers, N. A., R. K. Clifton, and M. G. Clarkson. 1987. When they were very young: Almost-threes remember two years ago. *Infant Behavior and Development*, 10: 123–132.

Paulson, G., and G. Gottlieb. 1968. Developmental reflexes: The reappearance of fetal and neonatal reflexes in aged patients. *Brain*, 91: 37–52.

Piaget, J. 1952. *The origins of intelligence in children.* New York: International Universities Press.

Piaget, J. 1954. *The construction of reality in the child.* New York: Ballantine Books.

Piaget, J. 1962. *Play, dreams and imitation in childhood.* New York: Norton.

Prechtl, H. F. R. 1977. *The neurological examination of the full term newborn infant.* Clinics in Developmental Medicine, no. 63. London: Heinemann.

Prechtl, H. F. R. 1981. The study of neural development as a perspective of clinical problems. In K. J. Conally & H. F. R. Prechtl, eds., *Maturation and development: Biological and psychological perspectives.* London: Heinemann.

Rader, N., and J. D. Stern. 1982. Visually elicited reaching in neonates. *Child Development,* 53: 1004–1007.

Ramey, C. T., and L. L. Ourth. 1971. Delayed reinforcement and vocalization rates of infants. *Child Development,* 42: 291–297.

Rheingold, H. L., J. L. Gewirtz, and H. W. Ross. 1959. Social conditioning of vocalizations in the infant. *Journal of Comparative and Physiological Psychology,* 52: 68–73.

Rheingold, H. L., and C. O. Eckerman. 1969. The infant's free entry into a new environment. *Journal of Experimental Child Psychology,* 8: 271–283.

Rovee, C. K., and D. T. Rovee. 1969. Conjugate reinforcement of infant exploration behavior. *Journal of Experimental Child Psychology,* 8: 33–39.

Rovee-Collier, C. K., M. W. Sullivan, M. Enright, D. Lucas, and J. Fagen. 1980. Reactivation of infant memory. *Science,* 208: 1159–1161.

Rubenstein, S. 1967. Maternal attentiveness and subsequent exploratory behavior in the infant. *Child Development,* 38: 1089–1100.

Ruff, H. A., and A. Malton. 1978. Is there directed reaching in the human neonate? *Developmental Psychology,* 14: 425–426.

Siqueland, E. R., and C. A. DeLucia. 1969. Visual reinforcement of nonnutritive sucking in human infants. *Science,* 165: 1144–1146.

Slater, A., V. Morison, and D. Rose. 1984. Habituation in the newborn. *Infant Behavior and Development,* 7: 183–200.

Sullivan, M. W., and M. Lewis. 1988. Facial expressions during learning in 1-year-old infants. *Infant behavior and development,* 11: 369–373.

Tamis-LeMonda, C. S., and M. H. Bornstein. 1989. Habituation and maternal encouragement of attention in infancy as predictors of toddler language, play and representational competence. *Child Development*, 60: 738–751.

Thelen, E., and D. M. Fisher. 1982. Newborn stepping: An explanation of a "disappearing" reflex. *Developmental Psychology*, 18: 706–715.

Ungerer, J. A., L. R. Brody, and P. R. Zelazo. 1978. Long-term memory for speech in 2-to-4-week-old infants. *Infant Behavior and Development*, 1: 177–186.

Von Hofsten, C. 1984. Developmental changes in the organization of prereaching movements. *Developmental Psychology*, 20: 378–388.

Vygotsky, L. S. 1978. *Mind in society*. Cambridge: Harvard University Press.

Watson, J. S., and C. T. Ramey. 1972. Reactions to response-contingent stimulation in early infancy. *Merrill-Palmer Quarterly*, 18: 323–340.

Yarrow, L. J., J. L. Rubenstein, F. A. Pedersen, and J. J. Jankowski. 1972. Dimensions of early stimulation and their different effects on infant development. *Merrill-Palmer Quarterly*, 18: 205–218.

Zelazo, P. R. 1976. From reflexive to instrumental behavior. In L. P. Lipsitt, ed., *Developmental psychology: The significance of infancy*. Hillsdale, N.J.: Erlbaum.

4 / EMOTIONS, INTERACTIONS, AND ATTACHMENTS

Achenbach, T. M. 1980. DSM-III in light of empirical research on the classification of child psychopathology. *Journal of the American Academy of Child Psychiatry*, 19: 395–412.

Ainsworth, M. D. S., and B. A. Wittig. 1969. Attachment and exploratory behavior of one-year-olds in a strange situation. In B. M. Foss, ed., *Determinants of infant behavior*, vol. 4. London: Methuen.

Aronson, E., and S. Rosenbloom. 1971. Space perception in early infancy: Perception within a common auditory space. *Science*, 172: 1161–1163.

Bates, J., et al. 1985. Pp. 167–193 in I. Bretherton and D.

Waters, eds., *Growing points in attachment theory and research*. Monographs of the Society for Research in Child Development, 50. Chicago: University of Chicago Press.

Blehar, M. C., A. F. Lieberman, and M. D. S. Ainsworth. 1977. Early face-to-face interaction and its relation to later infant-mother attachment. *Child Development*, 48: 182–194.

Bowlby, J. 1969. *Attachment and loss*, vol 1: *Attachment*. New York: Basic Books.

Brazelton, T. B., B. Koslowski, and M. Main. 1974. The origins of reciprocity: The early mother-infant interaction. In M. Lewis and L. A. Rosenblum, eds., *The effect of the infant on its caregiver*. New York: Wiley.

Bronson, G. W. 1972. *Infants' reactions to unfamiliar persons and novel objects*. Monographs of the Society for Research in Child Development, 37 (3, ser. no. 148). Chicago: University of Chicago Press.

Brooks, J., and M. Lewis. 1976. Infants' responses to strangers: Midget, adult, and child. *Child Development*, 4: 323–332.

Campos, J. J., and C. Stenberg. 1981. Perception, appraisal, and emotion: The onset of social referencing. Pp. 273–314 in M. Lamb and L. Sherrod, eds., *Infant social cognition*. Hillsdale, N.J.: Erlbaum.

Carpenter, G. C., J. J. Tecce, G. Stechler, and S. Friedman. 1970. Differential visual behavior to human and humanoid faces in early infancy. *Merrill-Palmer Quarterly*, 16: 91–108.

DeCasper, A. J., and W. P. Fifer. 1980. Of human bonding: Newborns prefer their mothers' voices. *Science*, 208: 1174–1176.

Donovan, W. L., and L. A. Leavitt. 1989. Maternal self-efficacy and infant attachment: Integrating physiology perceptions and behavior. *Child Development*, 60: 460–472.

Emde, R. N., D. H. Kligman, J. H. Reich, and T. O. Wade. 1978. Emotional expression in infancy: Initial studies of social signaling and an emergent model. In M. Lewis and

L. A. Rosenblum, eds., *The development of affect.* New York: Plenum.

Feinman, S., and M. Lewis. 1982. "Infant temperament and social referencing." Paper presented at the International Conference on Infant Studies, Austin, Tex.

Fernald, A., and T. Simon. 1984. Expanded intonation contours in mothers' speech to newborns. *Developmental Psychology,* 20: 104–113.

Field, T. 1977a. Effects of early separation, interactive deficits and experimental manipulations of infant-mother face-to-face interaction. *Child Development,* 48: 763–771.

Field, T. 1977b. Maternal stimulation during infant feeding. *Developmental Psychology,* 13: 539–540.

Field, T. 1978. Interaction behaviors of primary versus secondary caretaker fathers. *Developmental Psychology,* 14: 183–184.

Field, T. 1979a. Differential behavior and cardiac response of three-month-old infants to a mirror and peer. *Infant Behavior and Development,* 2: 179–184.

Field, T. 1979b. Games parents play with normal and high-risk infants. *Child Psychiatry and Human Development,* 10: 41–48.

Field, T. 1979c. Infant behaviors directed toward peers and adults in the presence and absence of mother. *Infant Behavior and Development,* 2: 47–54.

Field, T. 1979d. Visual and cardiac responses to animate and inanimate faces by young term and preterm infants. *Child Development,* 50: 188–194.

Field, T. 1981. Gaze behavior of normal and high-risk infants during early interactions. *Journal of the American Academy of Child Psychology,* 20: 308–317.

Field, T. 1986. Affective responses to separation. In T. B. Brazelton and M. W. Yogman, eds., *Affective development in infancy.* Norwood, N.J.: Ablex.

Field, T. 1987. Interaction and attachment in normal and atypical infants. *Journal of Consulting and Clinical Psychology,* 55: 1–7.

Field, T., J. Dempsey, N. Hallock, and H. H. Shuman. 1978.

Mothers' assessments of the behavior of their infants. *Infant Behavior and Development,* 1: 156–167.

Field, T., and E. Ignatoff. 1981. Videotaping effects on play and interaction behaviors of low income mothers and their infants. *Journal of Applied Developmental Psychology,* 2: 227–236.

Field, T., A. M. Sostek, P. Vietze, and P. H. Liederman. 1981. *Culture and early interactions.* Hillsdale, N.J.: Lawrence Erlbaum Associates.

Field, T., and J. L. Roopnarine. 1982. Infant-peer interactions. In T. Field, A. Juston, H. Quay, and G. Finley, eds., *Review of human development.* New York: Wiley.

Field, T., T. Walden, S. Widmayer, and R. Greenberg. 1982. The early development of preterm discordant twin pairs: Bigger is not always better. *Infant Behavior and Development,* 5: 153–163.

Field, T., and T. Walden. 1982. Perception and production of facial expressions in infancy and early childhood. In H. Reese and L. Lipsitt, eds., *Advances in child development and behavior,* vol. 16. New York: Academic.

Field, T., R. Woodson, D. Cohen, R. Greenberg, R. Garcia, and D. Collins. 1983. Discrimination and imitation of facial expressions by term and preterm neonates. *Infant Behavior and Development,* 6: 485–490.

Field, T., R. Greenberg, R. Woodson, D. Cohen, and R. Garcia. 1984. Facial expressions during Brazelton neonatal assessments. *Infant Mental Health Journal,* 5: 61–71.

Field, T., D. Cohen, R. Garcia, and R. Greenberg. 1984. Mother-stranger face discrimination by the newborn. *Infant Behavior and Development,* 7: 19–26.

Field, T., and N. Vega-Lahr. 1984. Early interactions between craniofacial anomaly infants and their mothers. *Infant Behavior and Development,* 7: 537–540.

Field, T., D. Sandberg, T. A. Quetel, R. Garcia, and M. Rosario. 1985. Effects of ultrasound feedback on pregnancy anxiety, fetal activity and neonatal outcome. *Obstetrics and Gynecology,* 66: 575–578.

Field, T., N. Vega-Lahr, S. Goldstein, and F. Scafidi. 1987.

Face-to-face interaction behavior across early infancy. *Infant Behavior and Development*, 10: 117–122.

Fogel, A. 1980. Peer- versus mother-directed behavior in one- to three-month-old infants. *Infant Behavior and Development*, 2: 215–226.

Fogel, A., G. R. Diamond, B. H. Langhorst, and V. Demos. 1981. Affective and cognitive aspects of the two-month-old's participation in face-to-face interaction with its mother. In E. Tronick, ed., *Joint regulation of behavior*. Cambridge, England: Cambridge University Press.

Fogel, A., S. Toda, and M. Kawai. 1988. Mother-infant face-to-face interaction in Japan and the United States: A laboratory comparison using three-month-old infants. *Developmental Psychology*, 24: 398–406.

Fox, N. A. 1985. Sweet/sour–interest/disgust: The role of approach-withdrawal in the development of emotions. In T. Field and N. Fox, eds., *Social perception in infancy*. Norwood, N.J.: Ablex.

Gewirtz, J. L., and M. Nogueras. 1988. "Do infant protests/distress during maternal departures and separations have a learned basis? How mothers contribute to their children's separation difficulties." Paper presented at the biennial International Conference on Infant Studies, Washington, D.C.

Gewirtz, J. L., and M. Palaez-Nogueras. 1989. "Maternal training of infant protests to discriminate between departure and separation settings." Paper presented at the biennial meeting of the Society for Research in Child Development, Kansas City, Mo.

Goldberg, S., S. Brachfeld, and B. DeVitto. 1980. Feeding, fussing, and playing: Parent-infant interaction in the first year as a function of prematurity and prenatal problems. In T. Field, S. Goldberg, D. Stern, and A. Sostek, eds., *High-risk infants and children: Adult and peer interactions*. New York: Academic Press.

Goldsmith, H. H., D. L. Bradshaw, and L. A. Rieser-Danner. 1986. Temperament and social interaction in infants and children. Pp. 5–34 in J. V. Lerner and R. M. Lerner, eds.,

New directions in child development, vol. 31. San Francisco: Jossey-Bass.

Gusella, J. L., D. Muir, and E. Z. Tronick. 1988. The effect of manipulating maternal behavior during an interaction on three- and six-month-olds' affect and attention. *Child Development,* 59: 1111–1124.

Haviland, J. M., and M. Lelucia. 1987. The induced affect response: ten-week-old infants' responses to three emotion expressions. *Developmental Psychology,* 23: 62–67.

Hiatt, S. W., J. J. Campos, and R. N. Emde. 1979. Facial patterning and infant emotional expression: Happiness, surprise, and fear. *Child Development,* 50: 1020–1035.

Hornik, R., and M. R. Gunnar. 1988. A descriptive analysis of infant social referencing. *Child Development,* 55(3): 626–634.

Hutt, C., and C. Ounsted. 1966. The biological significance of gaze aversion with particular reference to the syndrome of infantile autism. *Behavioral Science,* 11: 346–356.

Izard, C. E., R. R. Heuber, D. Risser, G. C. McGinnes, and L. M. Dougherty. 1980. The young infants' ability to produce discrete emotion expressions. *Developmental Psychology,* 16: 132–140.

Jones, O. 1980. Mother-child communication in very young Down's syndrome and normal children. In T. Field, S. Goldberg, D. Stern, and A. Sostek, eds., *High-risk infants and children: Adult and peer interactions.* New York: Academic.

Kaye, K. 1977. Toward the origin of dialogue. In H. R. Schaffer, ed., *Studies in mother-infant interaction.* New York: Academic.

Korner, A. F., C. H. Zlanak, J. Linden, R. I. Berkowitz, H. C. Kraemer, and W. S. Agras. 1985. The relation between neonatal and later activity and temperament. *Child Development,* 56: 38–42.

LaBarbera, J. D., C. E. Izard, P. Vietze, and S. A. Parisi. 1976. Four- and six-month-old infants' visual responses to joy, anger, and neutral expressions. *Child Development,* 47: 535–538.

Lamb, M. 1978. The development of sibling relationships in infancy: A short-term longitudinal study. *Child Development*, 49: 1189–1196.

Landau, R. 1989. Affect and attachment: Kissing, hugging and attachment behaviors. *Infant Mental Health Journal*, 10: 59–69.

Legerstee, M., A. Pomerleau, G. Malcuit, and H. Fieder. 1987. The development of infants' responses to peers and a doll: Implications for research in communication. *Infant Behavior and Development*, 10: 81–95.

Lester, B. M., J. Hoffman, and T. B. Brazelton. 1985. The rhythmic structure of mother-infant interaction in term and preterm infants. *Child Development*, 56: 15–27.

Lewis, M., and S. Goldberg. 1969. Perceptual-cognitive development in infancy: A generalized expectancy model as a function of the mother-infant interaction. *Merrill-Palmer Quarterly*, 5: 81–100.

Lewis, M., G. Young, J. Brooks, and L. Michalson. 1975. The beginning of friendship. In M. Lewis and L. Rosenblum, eds., *Friendship and peer relations*. New York: Wiley.

Londerville, S., and M. Main. 1981. Security of attachment, compliance and maternal training method in the second year of life. *Developmental Psychology*, 17: 289–299.

Ludemann, P. M., and C. A. Nelson. 1988. Categorical representation of facial expressions by seven-month-olds. *Developmental Psychology*, 24: 492–501.

Matheny, A. P., M. L. Riese, and R. J. Wilson. 1985. Rudiments of infant temperament: Newborn to nine months. *Developmental Psychology*, 21: 486–494.

Morgan, G. A. 1973. "Determinants of infants' reactions to strangers." Paper presented at the biennial meeting of the Society for Research in Child Development, Philadelphia.

Nimio, A., and N. Rinott. 1988. Fathers' involvement in the care of their infants and their attributions of cognitive competence to infants. *Child Development*, 59: 652–663.

Oster, H., and P. Ekman. 1978. Facial behavior in child development. In *Minnesota Symposium on Child Psychology*, vol. 2. Minneapolis: University of Minnesota Press.

Papousek, H., and M. Papousek. 1974. Mirror image and self-recognition in young human infants: A new method of experimental analysis. *Developmental Psychology*, 1: 149–157.

Parke, R. D., and S. O'Leary. 1975. Father-mother-infant interaction in the newborn period: Some findings, some observations, and some unresolved issues. In K. Riegel and J. Meacham, eds., *The developing individual in a changing world*. Social and Environmental Issues, 2. The Hague: Mouton.

Petrovich, S. B., J. L. Gewirtz, and D. T. Cerritti. 1989. "The role of learning in the infant fear-of-strangers phenomenon." Unpublished paper.

Plomin, R. 1982. Behavioral genetics and temperament. In R. Porter and G. M. Collins, eds., *Temperamental differences in infants and young children* (CIBA Foundation Symposium 89). London: Pitman.

Riese, M. L. 1987. Temperament stability between the neonatal period and twenty-four months. *Developmental Psychology*, 23: 216–222.

Robertson, J., and J. Robertson. 1971. Young children in brief separation. *Psychoanalytic Study of the Child*, 26: 264–315.

Robson, K. S. 1967. The role of eye-to-eye contact in maternal-infant attachment. *Journal of Child Psychology and Psychiatry*, 8: 13–15.

Roe, J. M., S. S. Feldman, and A. Drivas. 1988. Interactions with three-month-old infants: A comparison between Greek mothers and institutional caregivers. *International Journal of Behavioral Development*, 11: 359–367.

Rothbart, M. K. 1986. Longitudinal observation of infant temperament. *Developmental Psychology*, 22: 356–365.

Rothbart, M. K., and D. Derryberry. 1981. Development of individual differences in temperament. Pp. 383–400 in M. E. Lamb and A. L. Brown, eds., *Advances in developmental psychology*. New York: Medical and Scientific Books.

Sai, F., and I. W. R. Bushness. 1988. The perception of faces in different poses by one-month-olds. *Journal of Developmental Psychology*, 6: 35–41.

Sigman, M., C. Neumann, E. Carter, T. J. Cattle, S. D'Souza, and N. Birbo. 1988. Home interactions and the development of Embu toddlers in Kenya. *Child Development*, 59: 1251–1261.

Sorce, J. F., R. N. Emde, J. J. Campos, and M. D. Klinnert. 1985. Maternal emotional signaling: Its effect on the visual cliff behavior of one-year-olds. *Developmental Psychology*, 20: 195–200.

Sostek, A. M., and T. F. Anders. 1977. Relationships among the Brazelton Neonatal Scale, Bayley Infant Scales, and early temperament. *Child Development*, 48: 320–323.

Sostek, A. M., P. Vietze, M. Zaslow, L. Kreiss, F. ven der Waals, and D. Rubenstein. 1981. Social context in caregiver-infant interaction: A film study of FAIS and the United States. In Field et al. 1981.

Spitz, R. 1946. Anaclitic depression. *Psychoanalytic Study of the Child*, 2: 113–117.

Sroufe, L. A., and J. P. Wunsch. 1972. The development of laughter in the first year of life. *Child Development*, 43: 1326–1344.

Stechler, G., and G. Carpenter. 1967. A viewpoint on early affective development. In J. Hellmuth, eds., *The exceptional infant*, vol. 1. Seattle: Special Child Publications.

Stern, D. N. 1974. Mother and infant at play. In M. Lewis and J. Rosenblum, eds., *The effect of the infant on its caregiver*. New York: Wiley.

Termine, N. T., and C. E. Izard. 1988. Infants' responses to their mothers' expressions of joy and sadness. *Developmental Psychology*, 24: 223–229.

Trevarthen, C. 1974. Conversations with a two-month-old. *New Scientist*, 28: 230–233.

Trevarthen, C. 1985. Facial expressions of emotion in mother-infant interaction. *Human Neurobiology*, 4: 21–32.

Tronick, E., H. Als, L. Adamson, S. Wise, and T. B. Brazelton. 1978. The infant's response to entrapment between contradictory messages in face-to-face interaction. *Journal of Child Psychiatry*, 17: 1–13.

Tronick, E. Z., and J. F. Cohn. 1990. Infant-mother face-to-face interaction: Age and gender differences in coordination and the occurrence of miscoordination. In press.

Walden, T. A., and T. A. Ogan. 1988. The development of social referencing. *Child Development*, 59: 1230–1240.

Watson, J. S. 1967. Memory and "contingency analysis" in infant learning. *Merrill-Palmer Quarterly*, 13: 55–76.

Yogman, N. W., S. Dixon, E. Tronick, L. Adamson, H. Als, and T. B. Brazelton. 1976. "Development of infant social interaction with fathers." Paper presented at Eastern Psychological Association meeting, New York City.

5 / PEER INTERACTIONS AND DAYCARE

Barglow, P. 1987. Some further comments about infant daycare research. *Zero to Three*, 7: 26–28.

Belsky, J. 1986. Infant daycare: A cause for concern? *Zero to Three*, 6: 107.

Belsky, J. 1987. Is daycare bad for babies? *Time*, June 22, p. 63.

Blurton-Jones, N., and G. M. Leach. 1972. Behavior of children and their mothers at separation and greeting. In N. Blurton-Jones, ed., *Ethological studies of child behavior*. London: Cambridge University Press.

Chess, S. 1987. Comments. Infant daycare: A cause for concern: *Zero to Three*, 7: 24–25.

Eckerman, C. O., J. L. Whatley, and S. L. Kutz. 1975. Growth of social play with peers during the second year of life. *Developmental Psychology*, 11: 42–49.

Farber, E. A., and B. Egeland. 1982. Developmental consequences of out-of-home care for infants in a low income population. Pp. 102–125 in E. Zigler and E. Gordon, eds., *Day care.*

Field, T. 1979a. Differential behavioral and cardiac response of three-month-old infants to a mirror and a peer. *Infant Behavior and Development*, 2: 179–184.

Field, T. 1979b. Infant behaviors directed toward peers and

adults in the presence and absence of mother. *Infant Behavior and Development*, 2: 47–54.

Field, T. 1981. Gaze behavior of normal and high-risk infants during early interactions. *Journal of the American Academy of Child Psychiatry*, 20: 308–317.

Field, T. 1984. Separations of children attending new schools. *Developmental Psychology*, 20: 786–792.

Field, T. 1986. Affective responses to separation. In T. B. Brazelton and M. W. Yogman, eds. *Affective development in infancy*. New Jersey: Ablex.

Field, T. 1990. Grade school performance following infant daycare. In review.

Field, T., and J. L. Roopnarine. 1982. Infant-peer interactions. In T. Field, A. Huston, H. Quay, and G. Finley, eds., *Review of human development*. New York: Wiley.

Field, T., J. L. Gewirtz, D. Cohen, R. Garcia, R. Greenberg, and K. Collins. 1984. Leave-takings and reunions of infants, toddlers, preschoolers, and their parents. *Child Development*, 55: 628–635.

Field, T., N. Vega-Lahr, and S. Jagadish. 1986. Separation stress of nursery school infants and toddlers graduating to new classes. *Infant Behavior and Development*, 7: 277–284.

Field, T., W. Masi, S. Goldstein, S. Perry, and S. Parl. 1988. Infant daycare facilitates preschool social behavior. *Early Childhood Research Quarterly*, 3: 341–359.

Fogel, A. 1980. Peer vs. mother-directed behavior in one- to three-month-old infants. *Infant Behavior and Development*, 2: 215–226.

Fox, N., and T. Field. 1989. Individual differences in preschool entry behavior. *Journal of Applied Developmental Psychology*, 9: 211–216.

Haskins, R. 1985. Public school aggression among children with varying day-care experience. *Child Development*, 56: 689–703.

Howes, C. 1988. Peer interaction of young children. *Monographs of the Society for Research in Child Development*, 53.

Lewis, M., G. Young, J. Brooks, and L. Michalson. 1975. The beginning of friendship. In M. Lewis and L. Rosenblum, eds., *Friendship and peer relations*. New York: Wiley.

Mueller, E., and J. Brenner. 1977. The origins of social skills and interacting among playgroup toddlers. *Child Development*, 48: 854–861.

Oppenheim, D., A. Sagi, and M. E. Lamb. 1988. Infant-adult attachments on the kibbutz and their relation to socioemotional development four years later. *Developmental Psychology*, 24: 427–433.

Phillips, D., K. McCartney, S. Scarr, and C. Howes. 1987. Selective review of infant daycare research: A cause for concern? *Zero to Three*, 7: 18–21.

Roopnarine, J., and T. Field. 1983. Peer-directed behaviors of infants and toddlers during nursery school play. *Infant Behavior and Development*, 6: 133–138.

Rubenstein, J., C. Howes, and P. Boyle. 1981. A two year follow-up of infants in community-based day care. *Journal of Child Psychology and Psychiatry*, 22: 209–218.

Rutter, M. 1981. *Maternal deprivation reassessed*. 2nd ed. Middlesex, England: Penguin Books.

Schwartz, J. C., G. Krolick, and R. G. Strickland. 1973. Effects of early day care experience on adjustment to a new environment. *American Journal of Orthopsychiatry*, 43: 340–348.

Schwartz, J. C., R. G. Strickland, and G. Krolick. 1974. Infant day care: Behavioral effects at preschool age. *Developmental Psychology*, 10: 502–506.

Tronick, E., S. W. Winn, and G. Morelli. 1990. The child-holding patterns of the Efe (Pygmies) of Zaire. In T. Field and T. B. Brazelton, eds., *Advances in touch*. New Brunswick, N.J.: Johnson & Johnson.

Vandell, D., K. Wilson, and N. Buchanan. 1980. Peer interaction in the first year of life: An examination of its structure, content, and sensitivity to toys. *Child Development*, 51: 481–488.

Weinraub, M., and M. Lewis. The determinants of children's responses to brief periods of maternal absence. *Mono-*

graphs of the Society for Research in Child Development, 42 (4, serial no. 172).

Young, G., and M. Lewis. 1979. Effects of familiarity and maternal attention on infant peer relations. *Merrill-Palmer Quarterly*, 2: 105–120.

Zigler, E., and N. W. Hall. 1988. Daycare and its effect on children: An overview for pediatric health professionals. *Developmental and Behavioral Pediatrics*, 9: 38–46.

6 / INFANTS AT RISK

Ammann, A. J. 1987. Pediatric acquired immunodeficiency syndrome. Pp. 17–23 in *AIDS: Information for the Practicing Physician*, vol. 1. American Medical Association.

Arena, J. M. 1979. Drug and chemical effects on mother and child. *Pediatric Annals*, 8: 690–697.

Bakeman, R., and J. Brown. 1980. Early interaction: Consequences for social and mental development at three years. *Child Development*, 51: 437–447.

Belman, A. L., G. Diamond, D. Dickson, D. Horoupian, J. Llena, G. Lantos, and A. Rubinstein. 1988. Pediatric acquired immunodeficiency syndrome. *American Journal of Diseases of Children*, 142: 29–35.

Bettes, B. A. 1988. Maternal depression and "motherese": Temporal and intonational features. *Child Development*, 59: 1089–1096.

Burns, K., J. Melamed, W. Burns, I. Chasnoff, and R. Hatcher. 1985. Chemical dependents and clinical depression in pregnancy. *Journal of Clinical Psychology*, 41: 851–854.

Burns, W. J., and K. A. Burns. 1988. Parenting dysfunction in chemically dependent women. In I. J. Chasnoff, ed., *Drugs, alcohol, pregnancy and parenting*. Boston: Kluwer.

Clark, G. N., and R. Seifer. 1983. Facilitating mother-infant communication: A treatment model for high-risk and developmentally delayed infants. *Infant Mental Health Journal*, 4: 67–82.

Cohn, J. F., R. Matias, E. Z. Tronick, D. Connell, and K. Lyons-Ruth. 1986. Face-to-face interactions of depressed mothers and their infants. Pp. 31–45 in E. Tronick and T. Field, eds., *Maternal depression and infant disturbances*. San Francisco: Jossey-Bass.

Cornell, E. M., and A. W. Gottfried. 1976. Intervention with premature human infants. *Child Development*, 47: 32–39.

Curran, J. W., H. W. Jaffe, A. M. Hardy, W. M. Morgan, R. M. Selik, and T. J. Dondero. 1988. Epidemiology of HIV infection and AIDS in the United States. *Science*, 239: 610–616.

Field, T. 1977. Effects of early separation, interactive deficits, and experimental manipulations on infant-mother face-to-face interaction. *Child Development*, 48: 763–771.

Field, T. 1983. Early interactions and interaction coaching of high-risk infants and parents. In M. Perlmutter, ed., *Development and policy concerning children with special needs*. The Minnesota Symposia on Child Psychology. Hillsdale, N.J.: Erlbaum.

Field, T. 1984. Early interactions between infants and their postpartum depressed mothers. *Infant Behavior and Development*, 7: 527–532.

Field, T. 1987. Affective and interactive disturbances in infants. In J. Osofsky, ed., *Handbook of infant development*. New York: Wiley.

Field, T., E. Ignatoff, S. Stringer, J. Brennan, R. Greenberg, S. Widmayer, and G. Anderson. 1982. Nonnutritive sucking during tube feeding: Effects on preterm neonates in an ICU. *Pediatrics*, 70: 381–384.

Field, T., J. Dempsey, and H. H. Shuman. 1983. Five-year follow-up of preterm respiratory distress syndrome and post-term postmaturity syndrome infants. In T. Field and A. Sostek, eds., *Infants born at risk: Physiological, perceptual and cognitive processes*. New York: Grune & Stratton.

Field, T., D. Sandberg, R. Garcia, N. Vega-Lahr, S. Goldstein, and L. Guy. 1985. Prenatal problems, postpartum depression, and early mother-infant interactions. *Developmental Psychology*, 12: 1152–1156.

Field, T., D. Sandberg, T. A. Quetel, R. Garcia, and M. Rosario. 1985. Effects of ultrasound feedback on pregnancy anxiety, fetal activity and neonatal outcome. *Obstetrics and Gynecology*, 66: 525–528.

Field, T., S. M. Schanberg, F. Scafidi, C. R. Bauer, N. Vega-Lahr, R. Garcia, J. Nystrom, and C. M. Kuhn. 1986. Tactile/kinesthetic stimulation effects on preterm neonates. *Pediatrics*, 77: 654–658.

Field, T., B. Healy, S. Goldstein, S. Perry, D. Bendell, S. Schanberg, E. A. Zimmerman, and C. Kuhn. 1988. Infants of depressed mothers show "depressed" behavior even with non-depressed adults. *Child Development*, 59: 1569–1579.

Finnegan, L. P. 1988. Drug addiction and pregnancy: The newborn. In I. J. Chasnoff, ed., *Drugs, alcohol, pregnancy and parenting*. Boston: Kluwer.

Fraiberg, S. 1974. Blind infants and their mothers: An examination of the sign system. In M. Lewis and L. A. Rosenblum, eds., *The effect of the infant on its caregiver*. New York: Wiley.

Gaensbauer, T. J., R. J. Harmon, L. Cytryn, and D. H. McKnew. 1984. Social and affective development in infants with a manic-depressive parent. *American Journal of Psychiatry*, 141: 223–229.

Gottfried, A. W., and J. L. Gaiter. 1985. *Infant stress under intensive care*. Baltimore: University Park Press.

Greenberg, N. H. 1971. A comparison of infant-mother interactional behavior in infants with atypical behavior and normal infants. In J. Hellmuth, ed., *Exceptional infant*, vol. 2. New York: Brunner/Mazel.

Householder, J., R. Hatcher, W. Burns, and I. Chasnoff. 1982. Infants born to narcotic-addicted mothers. *Psychological Bulletin*, 92(2): 453–468.

Hunt, J. V. 1981. Predicting intellectual disorders in childhood for preterm infants with birthweights below 1501 grams. In S. L. Friedman and M. Sigman, eds., *Preterm birth and psychological development*. New York: Academic Press.

Jones, O. H. M. 1977. Mother-child communication with prelinguistic Down's syndrome and normal infants. In H. R.

Shaffer, ed., *Studies in mother-infant interaction.* London: Academic Press.

Levy-Shiff, R., H. Sharir, and M. B. Mogilner. 1989. Mother- and father-preterm infant relationship in the hospital preterm nursery. *Child Development,* 60: 93–102.

Massie, H. N. 1978. The early natural history of childhood psychosis: Ten cases studied by analysis of family home movies of the infancies of the children. *Journal of the American Academy of Child Psychiatry,* 17: 29–45.

McGehee, I. J., and C. O. Eckerman. 1983. The preterm infant as a social partner: Responsive but unreadable. *Infant Behavior and Development,* 6: 461–470.

Minkoff, H., D. Nanda, R. Menez, and S. Fikrig. 1987. Pregnancies resulting in infants with acquired immunodeficiency syndrome or AIDS-related complex: Follow-up of mothers, children, and subsequently born siblings. *Obstetrics and Gynecology,* 69: 288–291.

Pierog, S., O. Chandavasu, and I. Wexter. 1977. Withdrawal symptoms in infants with the fetal alcohol syndrome. *Journal of Pediatrics,* 90: 630–633.

Radke-Yarrow, M., E. M. Cummings, L. Kuczynski, and M. Chapman. 1985. Patterns of attachment in two- and three-year-olds in normal families and families with parental depression. *Child Development,* 56: 884–893.

Rausch, P. B. 1981. Effects of tactile and kinesthetic stimulation on premature infants. *Journal of Obstetric, Gynecological, and Neonatal Nursing,* 11: 34–37.

Regan, D., F. M. Rudranf, and L. Finnegan. 1980. Parenting abilities in drug dependent women: The negative effects of depression. *Pediatric Research,* 14: 454.

Rice, R. 1977. Neurophysiological development in premature infants following stimulation. *Developmental Psychology,* 13: 69–76.

Sameroff, A., R. Seifer, and M. Zax. 1982. Early development of children at risk for emotional disorder. *Monographs of the Society for Research in Child Development,* serial no. 199, 47(7).

Sameroff, A. V., and R. Seifer. 1983. Familial risk and child competence. *Child Development*, 54: 1254–1268.

Scott, G. B., M. A. Fischl, N. Klimas, M. A. Fletcher, G. M. Dickenson, R. S. Levine, and W. P. Parks. 1985. Mothers of infants with acquired immunodeficiency syndrome. *Journal of the American Medical Association*, 253: 363–366.

Siegel, L. A. 1983. The prediction of possible learning disabilities in preterm and full-term children. In T. Field and A. Sostek, eds., *Infants born at risk: Physiological, perceptual and cognitive processes.* New York: Grune & Stratton.

Stanley, K., B. Soule, and S. A. Copans. 1979. Dimensions of prenatal anxiety and their influence on pregnancy outcome. *American Journal of Obstetrics and Gynecology*, 135: 333–348.

Stechler, G., and A. Halton. 1982. Prenatal influences on human development. In B. B. Wolman, ed., *Handbook of developmental psychology.* Englewood Cliffs, N.J.: Prentice-Hall.

Streissguth, A. P., et al. 1984. Intrauterine alcohol and nicotine exposure: Attention and reaction time in four-year-old children. *Developmental Psychology*, 20: 533–541.

Streissguth, A. P., et al. 1986. Attention, distraction and reaction time at age seven years and prenatal alcohol exposure. *Neurobehavioral Toxicology and Teratology*, 8: 717–725.

Streissguth, A. P., H. M. Barr, P. D. Sampson, B. L. Darby, and D. C. Martin. 1989. IQ at age four in relation to maternal alcohol use and smoking during pregnancy. *Developmental Psychology*, 25: 3–11.

White, J., and R. Labarba. 1976. The effects of tactile and kinesthetic stimulation on neonatal development in the premature infant. *Developmental Psychobiology*, 9: 569–577.

Widmayer, S., C. R. Bauer, and T. Field. In review. Affective disorders in children born with perinatal complications.

Wilson, G. W., K. McCraery, J. Keen, and J. Baxter. 1979. The development of preschool children of heroin-addicted mothers: A controlled study. *Pediatrics*, 63: 135–141.

Zahn-Waxler, C., E. M. Cummings, D. H. McKnew, and M.

Radke-Yarrow. 1984. Altruism, aggression, and social interactions in young children with a manic-depressive parent. *Child Development*, 55: 112–122.

AFTERWORD

Field, T. 1989. Infancy risk factors and risk-taking. *European Journal of Psychology of Education*, 4: 175–177.

Field, T., P. McCabe, and N. Schneiderman, eds. 1990. *Stress and coping during infancy and childhood*. Hillsdale, N.J.: Lawrence Erlbaum Associates.

Garmezy, N., and M. Rutter, eds. 1983. *Stress, coping, and development in children*. New York: McGraw-Hill.

Werner, E. 1988. Individual differences, universal needs: A thirty-year study of resilient high-risk infants. *Zero to Three*, 8: 1–5.

Illustration Sources

Photographs at chapter openings and previously unpublished illustrations were provided by the author.

1.1   Anthony DeCasper.
1.2   Charles Darwin. *The expression of the emotions
          in man and animals,* p. 147, plate 1. Chicago:
          University of Chicago Press, 1965.
1.3   A. N. Meltzoff. Imitation of facial and manual
          gestures by human neonates. *Science,* 198
          (1977): 75. Copyright 1977 by the AAAS.
2.2   J. Steiner. Human facial expressions in
          response to taste and smell stimulation. In H.
          Reese and L. P. Lipsett, eds., *Advances in child
          development and behavior,* pp. 257–295, figure 1.
          Orlando, Fla.: Academic Press, 1979.
2.3   T. Field et al. Cardiac and behavioral
          responses to repeated tactile and auditory
          stimulation by preterm and term neonates.
          Developmental Psychology, 15 (1979): 411.
          Copyright 1979 by the American Psychological
          Association. By permission of the publisher.
2.4   Goren et al. Visual following and pattern
          discrimination of facelike stimuli by newborn
          infants. *Pediatrics,* 56 (1975): 544–549.
2.5   T. Field et al. Discrimination and imitation of

facial expressions by neonates. *Science,* 218 (1982): 181. Copyright 1982 by the AAAS.

3.1, 3.2   J. Brooks-Gunn.

4.1   T. Field. Neonatal perception of people: Maturational and individual differences. In T. Field and N. Fox, eds., *Social perception in infants,* p. 44. Norwood, N.J.: Ablex Publishing Company, 1985.

4.3   T. Field. Behavioral and cardiovascular activity during interactions between "high risk" infants and adults. In J. Karoly and J. Steffen, eds., *Child health psychology,* p. 197. Oxford: Pergamon Press, 1982. Reprinted with permission.

4.4   M. Martini.

4.5   R. Greenberg.

5.1, 5.2, 5.3   T. Field. Affective responses to separation. In T. B. Brazelton and M. W. Yogman, eds., *Affective development in infancy.* Norwood, N.J.: Ablex Publishers, 1986.

6.1   T. Field et al. Tactile/kinesthetic stimulation effects on preterm neonates. *Pediatrics,* 77 (1986): 657. Reproduced by permission.

6.2, 6.3   T. Field et al. Behavior state matching in mother-infant interactions of nondepressed versus depressed mother-infant dyads. *Developmental Psychology,* 26 (1990): 7–14. Copyright 1990 by the American Psychological Association. By permission of the publisher.

Index

Accommodation, 52–53

Activity level: and separation, 97, 98; depressed mothers and, 119. *See also* Hyperactivity

Activity records, 13

Adjustment, daycare and, 93–96

Affect. *See* Emotions

Affection, physical, and peer attachment, 97, 98

Age-appropriate infant games, 72

Age differences, in interaction behavior, 68

Aggressiveness: daycare and, 90, 91–92, 93; and separation, 97, 98, 99

AIDS, 104

Alcohol, and prenatal risk, 107–109

Amniotic fluid, 19

Anal stage, 3

Animation, in stimuli, 7, 9–10, 67

Anxiety, maternal, 109–110

Apgar test, 24

Apnea, 112

Assimilation, 52–53

Attachment: person permanence and, 54; to parents, 77–83, 85, 91, 100–101; disorders, 78; and separation stress, 80–83, 97–101; day-care and, 90–91, 93, 97–101; peer, 97–101

Attention: measuring, 6–8; and interesting stimuli, 9–10; and medication at birth, 21; neonatal, 39; early interaction disturbances and, 122

Autistic children, 71, 123

Avoidance, 90, 91. *See also* Gaze aversion

Babinski reflex, 43

Baby talk, 68, 69, 72

Balance: fetal sense of, 19; neonatal sense of, 29

Bayley scales, 11, 47, 55, 57, 114, 118

Beck Depression Inventory, 106

Behavior: reflex, 5, 18–19, 42–46; voluntary, 5, 46, 53; diaries of, 13; fetal, 17–21; interaction, 68, 86; visual, 70; familiar, 88; with fetal alcohol syndrome, 108; of preemies, 112–113; depressed, 120; disturbed interaction, 122–125; coping, 127. *See also* Infant response; Learning; Sensorimotor abilities

Behavioral disorganization, neonatal, 21, 42

Behavior disorders, 113, 122

163

651008

651